T0156591

But I Never Made a Loan
My Career in Banking – The Early Years

Carter H. Golembe

iUniverse, Inc.
New York   Bloomington

But I Never Made a Loan

iUniverse books may be ordered through booksellers or by contacting:

iUniverse
1663 Liberty Drive
Bloomington, IN 47403
www.iuniverse.com
1-800-Authors (1-800-288-4677)

ISBN: 978-1-4401-7475-9 (sc)
ISBN: 978-1-4401-7473-5 (dj)
ISBN: 978-1-4401-7474-2 (ebook)

Library of Congress Control Number: 2009912370

Printed in the United States of America

iUniverse rev. date: 11/18/2009

Acknowledgements

I am extremely grateful to my wife Patricia Healy-Golembe, who spent countless hours typing and retyping the manuscript over a period of six years. Without her inspiration, completion of this book would not have been possible.

Contents

Preface

"You ought to write a book about it." The "it" is my involvement in banking since the end of World War II, and the suggestion comes from friends and colleagues as well as from assorted family members, doubtless weary of my stories. My usual response has been that I could not write credibly about the banking business without ever having been a banker.

Of course, I have been writing and speaking about public policy issues in banking for many years, but bankers will understand my reservations in this instance. There is no greater divide in banking than that between those who have spent much of their careers deciding on the creditworthiness of potential borrowers and those who have not. Bank chief executive officers tend to come from the first group, not from the second. At least this was the way it was until very recently, when the barriers between banking and other financial businesses began to come down, but I expect it is still largely the case. Of the crucial assessments that could thwart the careers of potential bank presidents, there was never a more damning phrase than "but he never made a loan."

Obviously I have overcome my reservations. The title I selected is not only a confession, but also a warning to bankers who might think that this book will improve their banking skills or reveal valuable new banking strategies. It will not. This will still be left to bankers themselves, professional consultants, economists and lawyers – probably in that order.

Personally, I find banking to be an endlessly fascinating business, but too often described in terms of the number or size of banks, or of laws governing their activities or, the favorite I guess, of the occasional "banking panics" that dot our financial history. The real fascination of banking – I am almost tempted to use the word "romance" – stems from the fact that it is a people business conducted in a very large number of institutions by a very large number of persons, and it touches the lives of almost every individual in this nation. Banking has a record compiled by visionaries, practical men of affairs and rascals – some of them bankers and some of them bank supervisors. It has a history of solid performance, studded also with breath-taking accomplishments and ignominious failures. My objective is to tell just a part of the story as it unfolded during the past half century or so.

I am relying upon the fact that there is virtually no aspect of the banking business – other than the crucial job of extending credit – in which I have not been involved in some fashion or other since the end of World War II. Presumably this was one reason my friends kept insisting that it was time to put something down on paper. Over the years I taught banking and economic history at the college level, as well as at many of the banking industry's "graduate" schools (particularly the Pacific Coast Banking School at the University of Washington). I wrote several books on banking. I spent almost a decade on the staff of a federal banking agency (with a brief stint as a bank examiner). I served on the Senate payroll as a special assistant to a U.S. Senator during a major investigation of banking and monetary policy. I thoroughly enjoyed six years as a banking trade association executive. I founded a bank consulting firm and spent over 20 years as an advisor to major banks, following which I served for several years as the chairman of another prominent consulting firm. Overlapping much of the consulting period, I spent 10 years on the board of directors of one of the nation's largest bank holding companies (on the audit committee, no less). In recent years, I have focused on speaking before financial groups and on writing the monthly *Golembe Report* on public policy issues. I launched *The Golembe Reports* in 1967 and ceased publication 35 years later to begin writing this book.

It was in my role as a speaker that I have had to deal most often with the problem of being introduced as a banking "guru," which always causes me to think ruefully of someone's observation that the word "guru" only became useful and popular once headline writers realized that it contained fewer letters than charlatan.

A few comments on the format of this book may be useful. In the United States, banking is almost entirely in private hands and yet government, particularly but not solely at the federal level, is deeply involved in oversight and regulation. I have always found that the most interesting issues in banking arise out of the interplay between the private and public interests involved. This is the cord that holds together the story that follows.

It is remarkable that several important policy issues in the early 21st century are not very different from those that were with us 150 years ago. This does not mean that it is necessary to be a full-fledged historian to understand or deal with the controversies and the argumentation that one encounters nowadays. However, it is a definite advantage to come to them with some understanding of how we got to where we are at the present time. In banking, possibly more so than in any other industry, history counts.

In this book I will take readers along with me as I witnessed banking from various vantage points during my career, especially the decades of the 1950s and 1960s. Each of these "windows" afforded a special view of banking. For example, it appears quite different when one is regulating banks than when one is advising them on how to deal with regulators. And the view from Capitol Hill is not the same as from Wall Street. My hope is that readers will gain a reasonably good understanding of how U. S. banking came to be what it is.

The account that follows is not intended to be just about me or even mostly about me. It is autobiographical only to the extent necessary to explain why I saw banking in a certain way at each stage of my career. For those who are curious about banking, or who are puzzled by some of the things that have happened, or who simply want to know a little more about banking, this book may turn out to be interesting – possibly even provocative. I sincerely hope that even bankers may enjoy it.

Carter H. Golembe
Delray Beach, Florida

Foreword

I first met Carter Golembe in 1966 at the National Press Club when I was a young financial writer and editor. He was still a senior staffer with the American Bankers Association, but was about to launch *The Golembe Reports* and start his own banking research and consulting firm originally called Carter H. Golembe Associates, Inc. (later to become just Golembe Associates, Inc.). Little did I know that our introduction would lead to a treasured personal and professional relationship that has spanned more than 40 years – helping him with *The Golembe Reports,* working with him at two consulting firms and editing two of his book manuscripts. Much of my knowledge about U.S. banking structure and regulation I gained from Carter. I also have him to credit for my love of banking history.

So it is a pleasure and a privilege for me to serve as editor of this memoir and to write this foreword. The foreword is necessary because, for health reasons, Carter was unable to complete his plan of covering all phases of his distinguished career as a banking economist and consultant. This book deals with his career from 1951, when he joined the Federal Deposit Insurance Corporation, to 1966 when he left the ABA to establish Golembe Associates. Except for the final chapter, it does not deal with his career at Golembe Associates or thereafter.

Golembe Associates had a unique concept. It was created to provide professional consulting and research services "in the crucial area where economics, law and government meet to affect banking institutions," said the firm's first published annual report in 1974. "That basic concept enables the firm to offer a variety of services in addition to consulting and research, such as seminars, legislative monitoring and specialized training for banks." By the late 1980s, the firm had expanded into financial consulting, regulatory consulting and management consulting. Financial consulting included merger and acquisition structure and pricing, fairness opinions, branch sales and purchases, valuation studies, and merger and acquisition planning strategies. Regulatory consulting included merger and acquisition consulting, supervisory consulting, business plans and capital plans, special consulting on interstate banking, expert testimony, government affairs services, public policy consulting and public policy advisory services. Management consulting included strategic planning, market research and analysis, earnings enhancements, post-merger integration, organization and structure, payment systems consulting and trust department consulting.

Of course, Carter Golembe was the central figure in the firm. Indeed, for the first few years, he was the only full-time consultant on the staff in Washington, the firm's home base. He would develop business with banking institutions of all sizes – money-center banks, regional banks and, in notable cases, even small community banks – as well as with financial trade associations. Depending on the task at hand, he would enlist one or more of the part-time "associates," who were not based in Washington, to work with him on research or consulting projects. The initial group of associates was an impressive bunch – Donald P. Jacobs, Professor of Banking at Northwestern University (later Dean of Northwestern's famous Kellogg School of Management); Charles F. Haywood, Dean of the College of Commerce at the University of Kentucky; Gerald C. Fisher, Research Professor of Business Administration at Temple University; and Clifford H. Kreps, the Wachovia Professor of Banking at the University of North Carolina. All of them were well-known and respected in the fields of economics and finance. Carter hired his first full-time Washington consultant about 1970, and the professional staff began to expand slowly but surely. I joined the firm in 1972.

By 1974 the firm had assembled a wide array of clients. Its executive consulting clients, many of which engaged Golembe Associates in connection with strategic planning, were Alabama Bancorp of Birmingham, American Fletcher Corp of Indianapolis, Colonial Bank & Trust Co., of Waterbury, Conn., Equibank, N.A., of Pittsburgh, First Arkansas Bankstock Corp., of Little Rock, First Financial Group of Manchester, N.H., First National Bank of Louisville, Ky., Flagship Banks of Miami Beach, Fla., Marine Midland Banks of Buffalo, N.Y., New England Merchants National Bank of Boston, North Carolina National Bank of Charlotte, N.C., Northwest Bancorp of Minneapolis, Minn., Republic National Bank of Dallas, Tex., United Bank of Denver, Washington Trust Bank of Spokane and Winters National Bank & Trust Co., of Dayton, Ohio. All of these institutions have since gone through mergers and acquisitions, many times over in some cases. But the list includes a couple of notable survivors. For example, Bank of America in 2009 is operating under the charter of the North Carolina National Bank, which through its holding company (NCNB Corp and its successor) made many acquisitions prior to acquiring BofA. Meanwhile, what was once Northwest Bancorp., a regional banking power over many decades, became one of the nation's largest banking organizations through its acquisition of Wells Fargo Bank.

Golembe Associates also had legislative and special consulting clients of all shapes and sizes by 1974. They were the American Bankers Association, the Bank Marketing Association, Bankers Trust Co., of New York, the California Bankers Association, Charter New York Corporation, Chemical Bank of New York, the Conference of State Bank Supervisors, Continental Illinois Bank & Trust Co., of Chicago, First Union Group of St. Louis, Mo, Harris Trust & Savings Bank of Chicago, Mercantile Trust Co., of St. Louis, Mo., National Shawmut Bank of Boston, New Jersey National Corp., of Trenton, Northern Virginia Bank of Springfield, Va., Rochester Savings Bank & Trust of Rochester, N.H., Salomon Brothers of New York, Valley Bank & Trust of Chambersburg, Pa., and Valley National Bank of Phoenix, Ariz.

In addition, the firm had scores of other clients who belonged to one or more of the seminar groups managed by Golembe Associates. One was the Washington Seminar for Bank Executives, which originally consisted of 16 major banking organizations whose senior officers met to consider current and emerging public policy issues. Another was the Executive Seminars on Long-Range Planning, which originally consisted of 80 money-center and regional banks whose senior officers met to consider issues important to the long-range planning efforts of their organizations. A third was the Trust Research Seminars, which originally consisted of the senior trust officer from 10 of the 50 largest bank trust departments in the country. This seminar provided a forum for the discussion of serious research efforts on bank trust issues as well as legislative and regulatory developments affecting the trust industry. A fourth was the International Financial Conference, which originally provided a forum for senior bank officers from major regional banking organizations to consider public policy issues related to international banking. This seminar was typically conducted overseas. Also in the 1970s, Golembe Associates launched the National Conference on Competition in Banking, an organization of financial executives from across the country that acted as a continuing forum for informed discussion and analysis of anticompetitive constraints on banks and other depository institutions. This organization focused on such issues as interest rate controls, limits on geographic expansion and restrictions on product expansion.

From the beginning, Golembe Associates also maintained a continuing but modest publications program, including *The Golembe Reports*. One such publication was *Bank Expansion Quarterly*, which provided information and analysis on acquisitions and mergers, bank-related expansion and branching. Another was *Federal Regulation of Banking*, a non-legal text designed primarily for bankers and banking schools that covered the history and scope of banking regulation by the federal government. The original book was co-authored by Carter Golembe and Raymond E. Hengren. Later editions were co-authored by Carter and David S. Holland. *Banking Expansion Reporter,* published by Prentice Hall Law & Business, was added to the list of Golembe Associates publications in 1982. In addition, Carter and I co-authored regular monthly columns on banking structure and regulation for such magazines as the *United States Banker, Bank Marketing Magazine,* the *Illinois Banker* and the *Kentucky Banker.*

But the flagship of the firm's publications always was *The Golembe Reports. The Golembe Reports* were published on more or less a monthly basis from 1967 to 2002. They were not akin to magazine columns or newspaper op-ed articles, but were lengthy interpretative essays on major public policy issues affecting banking. As such, *The Golembe Reports* constitute the most valuable legacy Carter Golembe leaves to the field of banking history. Carter authored the vast majority of *The Golembe Reports* himself, although over the years he occasionally had guest-written editions. I had the privilege of writing a number of those and co-authoring others.

The affiliation of Golembe Associates with *The Golembe Reports* ended in 1989 when the firm was acquired by BEI Holdings, Ltd., an Atlanta-based diversified consulting, management services and real estate company offering a broad range of products to the financial services industry. At that time, Carter Golembe became Chairman of the Board of The Secura Group, another Washington-based bank consulting firm headed by former FDIC Chairman William M. Isaac. I soon followed Carter to Secura. Carter continued to write *The Golembe Reports* while at Secura and later in his own firm, CHG Consulting, Inc.

Carter is sometimes called the dean of banking consultants, and the title is richly deserved. This book may help you understand why.

Philip C. Meyer
Editor, *But I Never Made a Loan*

Introduction

The U.S. Banking System – And How It Got that Way

Selecting 35 years or so in the middle of the 20th century as an appropriate period for stories about banking in the United States is not as unusual as it might appear. The year 1950 was when the U.S. banking system pulled itself together and resumed full operation after the catastrophic Great Depression of the 1930s and the disruptions of World War II. It was also about the same time that I began my 50-year journey through the banking industry. A warning is necessary: what follows is not a full or complete history of U.S. banking since 1950. It is, rather, a commentary that explains significant events in banking. These events are those that I had been able to observe closely, often as a participant in some fashion or other. A great deal had happened in the banking industry after 1950, and much of that will not be found here. Still, I am an economic historian by trade and, therefore, am always seeking rational explanations for developments that are still thought to be mysterious or, even worse, those whose origins have been explained poorly or incorrectly. There are more than a few of these in the chapter that now follows.

The old banking system died with the failure of more than 9,000 banks during the banking crisis of 1930-33. Significant changes in the system began to surface even in the midst of the crisis. As the economist John Kenneth Galbraith put it: President Herbert Hoover, desperate over the Federal Reserve's unwillingness to fight the depression to the full extent of its power, decided that "a special lender of last resort had to be created [and] in 1932 the Reconstruction Finance Corporation was brought into existence." This was followed in the Roosevelt Administration by the creation of a slew of new financial agencies, one of the most important of which was the Federal Deposit Insurance Corporation (FDIC) in 1933. The near fatal ineptitude displayed by the Federal Reserve during the crisis did not lead to the Fed's demise, although it must have been a close call. Instead, it led to significant reform of the Federal Reserve System in the Banking Act of 1935, effectively creating a new and more powerful central bank. The reformed Federal

Reserve replaced the central bank of 1913, which by 1930 had become a loose confederation of regional barons, unable to act decisively or wisely in an emergency.

A lot of mopping up remained to be done once the crisis ended, most importantly by the FDIC because the depression lasted another five years or so. Then bank failures disappeared as the wartime economy took over. Before long, bank assets came to consist largely of U.S. Treasury bonds, fixed in price by the Federal Reserve. The annual number of bank failures declined precipitously to just a few per year. In 1945, possibly for the first time ever in U.S. history, only a single bank failure occurred – and this was to happen on a few other occasions during the next several decades. The Federal Deposit Insurance Act of 1950 provided for some reduction of insurance assessments when insurance losses were low, doubled deposit insurance coverage from $5,000 to $10,000 and, largely as a symbolic action but still welcomed by the FDIC, provided that the law governing FDIC operations would be removed from the Federal Reserve Act and henceforth be known as the Federal Deposit Insurance Act. Then, early in 1951, the Treasury and the Federal Reserve reached their historic "accord," bringing the Federal Reserve out from under its wartime subservience to the Treasury Department. Thus, 1950 becomes the logical year to pick up the story of the evolving U.S. banking system, then already 150 years old.

Evolution of the U.S. Banking System. Imagine a U.S. banker who, like Rip Van Winkle, had fallen asleep more than 50 years ago and had just awakened. I doubt that this present-day Rip would have much difficulty getting his bearings, indeed might feel quite at home. Most of the pieces of the landscape with which he had been familiar were still in place. Looking at the banking system of 2005, for example, Rip would certainly recognize the major characteristics – an exceptionally large number of banks and a system offering newcomers to banking (as it had ever since 1863) the choice of either a federal or state charter for a commercial bank. Banks were still supervised by at least one of the three major federal banking agencies plus, if a state-chartered bank, the state's own banking department.

As was the case more than a half-century earlier, only one of the federal agencies has sole responsibility for chartering, supervising, and, when necessary, closing commercial banks (the Comptroller of the Currency in the case of national banks only). The other two federal agencies – the FDIC and the Federal Reserve – have no bank chartering powers, but have a certain involvement in the supervision of national banks, all of which are members of the Federal Reserve System and have deposits insured by the FDIC. The Fed and the FDIC share with state authorities supervisory responsibilities with respect to state-chartered banks, with the division between them depending on whether the state banks have become members of the Federal Reserve System, or have not joined the System but still have deposits insured by the FDIC. In fact, because most U.S. banks are state-chartered and relatively few other than the larger state banks opt for Fed membership, the greatest number of banks in the United States is still supervised by the FDIC. However, the bulk of U.S. banking assets are in national banks supervised directly by the Comptroller of the Currency and in state member banks of the Federal Reserve System.

It is often said, and even believed by many bankers, that the United States has a "dual banking system," meaning separate systems for state and national banks. This was true from 1863, when the dual system was created, until 1913, when the Federal Reserve was established. Today, the three federal banking agencies are in virtually full control, with only negligible (but still quite expensive) face-saving exceptions maintained for the benefit of state authorities. The once-accurate picture of a state system experimenting to its heart's content with banking powers, and free to decide who could enter the banking business under state charter, is gone. The final decision in such cases, as in almost all other significant matters, is made by a federal agency. To be sure, a few state banking agencies continue to play an influential role, although it is difficult to think of many beyond the New York State Banking Department. Most of this was true before our Rip had begun his long sleep, so that he would not have registered any surprise when awakening.

As in the past, our Rip would find that the *American Banker* continues to report daily on the wrestling and bickering among banks large and small, and between banks and the regulatory agencies, over the powers of banks and other financial institutions. And he would see the public's attitude toward banking more skeptical than ever as the financial crisis of the last half of the century's first decade deepened. Personally, I am still waiting for the first Hollywood epic that will have a banker as its hero, but that probably won't happen anytime soon. Thus far, the closest that Hollywood ever came to this was Jimmy Stewart's classic *It's A Wonderful Life*, but even there close observers would quickly remind us that Stewart was cast as the head of a savings and loan association and not a bank.

Of course, our modern-day Rip Van Winkle would soon become aware of certain important changes that had taken place while he was asleep. For example, there was the great technological revolution that began about 1950. And there was the virtual disappearance of the savings and loan industry, a victim of the sky-high inflation of the 1980s combined with the industry's serious miss-match of assets and with the inability of the Federal Savings and Loan Insurance Corporation (FSLIC) to close failed institutions and pay creditors because it lacked the funds to do so. To be sure, thrift institutions of various types are still around, but the FSLIC had to be taken over by the FDIC, and the once politically dominant, all-powerful, U.S. Savings & Loan League is no more.

It could not have taken Rip very long to notice in 2005 that there were fewer banks in the United States. When he fell asleep in 1950 there were about 13,500 insured commercial banks, compared to "only" about 7,000-8,000 in 2005. Moreover, there are an increasing number of very large banks. This was not because of a gigantic wave of bank failures and enforced bank consolidations such as occurred in the Great Depression of 1930-33. The more recent decline came about because of the repeal of federal statutes, mostly in the 1990s, which had strictly limited intrastate and interstate branching or interstate holding company operations so that many more bank mergers or holding company acquisitions became possible. But the inherent vigor of our unique banking system was still apparent. For example, in the 10 years that ended in 2004, 1,500 new banks were chartered in the United States, easily twice the combined total of all banks operating in Britain, Japan and Canada. In *Banking Regulation in the United States*, Professor Carl Felsenfeld of Fordham University's Law School observed that: "Despite the declining number of banks, the United States is the most over-banked [country] in the world."

Legislation of major importance to the banking system was rare during the most recent half-century if one ignores, as I do, the flurry of costly consumer protection laws, beginning about 1968, which always seemed to have titles beginning with "Fair," "Truth," "Equal" or "Community" and if we cut through the hype given to other pieces of legislation, such as the Gramm-Leach-Bliley Act, the 1999 statute supposedly designed to "modernize" banking law. But there was one towering exception: the Bank Holding Company Act Amendments of 1970, which was to have, and is still exerting, a profound effect on the banking system. The original Bank Holding Company Act of 1956 applied only to companies owning two or more banks and strictly limited their non-banking activities. The 1970 amendments to that law brought one-bank holding companies under regulation as well and expanded the permissible non-banking activities of bank holding companies to include those deemed "so closely related to banking or managing or controlling banks as to be a proper incident thereto."

If commentators and students of the U.S. banking system could be said to agree on any single point, it would be that the system now in place is absurdly complex and inefficient. Most prestigious groups that have examined the system since the final major piece was locked into place with the creation of the FDIC in 1933 have reached this conclusion. One of the most thorough studies, in my opinion, was made more than 40 years ago by Howard

H. Hackley, the General Counsel of the Federal Reserve Board. Hackley concluded that we have a system of "almost unbelievable complexity," giving rise "not only to great confusion," but also to "competitive inequalities." In short, he said: "It is a banking system that works," but one that no one could honestly say "works well." Since 1966, when Mr. Hackley wrote his article, working relationships between and among the various government agencies, which had been a major problem during the preceding six or seven years, have been improved. But this might not be saying much because in 1966 these relationships had probably reached their lowest possible level.

Rather clearly, Hackley found a quite unsatisfactory banking system, as have many other commentators. Nevertheless, if the U.S. banking system today is compared with that about which Hackley wrote, many would conclude – and I am one – that the earlier system comes off almost as a model of simplicity, clarity and efficiency.

A Product of Patchwork Fixes. According to almost everyone, the banking structure we have in the early 21st century was simply an accident. For over 200 years Congress, sometimes with the support of the banking industry and sometimes over its opposition, had enacted legislation that, at the time, seemed well-intentioned, and often much needed, to deal with problems in the banking system. But, so the story goes, the legislation lacked a guiding set of principles. Given the apparent inability of Congress to focus on long-term banking issues, the result was simply to continue to pile new legislation on top of old, leaving the U.S. with a system for which there is seemingly no coherent or logical plan.

This characterization of the present banking structure is the starting point for virtually every effort behind major reform. Such attempts usually begin with charts displaying the overlapping or conflicting responsibilities of the regulatory agencies. In fact, to anyone studying these charts, it is quite obvious that the banking system cannot work. Yet like the bumblebee, which experts in aerodynamics tell us should not be able to fly (but it does), so, too, the U.S. banking system should be unable to function (but it has, and does). It works because experienced professionals, sometimes willingly and sometimes out of sheer frustration, make the necessary arrangements and concessions to see that it works. Whether it works really well remains a question.

Reform of the banking system and its regulatory structure has been a "work in progress" since at least 1933. According to a paper prepared by the FDIC for a Washington conference that it hosted in March 2003, there have been 24 major proposals for reforming the banking system during the past 70 years by prestigious government and private organizations, including two Presidential Commissions. But these produced no acceptable answers to such questions as which federal agencies should be elevated, or combined with others, or merged out of existence. Nor did they foster agreement on whether new agencies should replace any or all of the present agencies. Bits and pieces of several of the 24 studies eventually did lead to some useful changes in existing law, but not one led to fundamental reform.

This record, in my opinion, is pretty strong evidence that the existing banking system and structure, with all of its faults, is surprisingly strong. One does not expect a "jerry-built" structure, as the present system is often described, to be able to stand up against powerful assaults from Congress, prestigious "think tanks" and noted academics. That it has survived at all calls for a brief foray into the fascinating story of early American banking.

In the United States, banking did not evolve naturally and smoothly out of a preexisting system, nor did it have European examples to follow. Instead, U.S. banking emerged full-blown with independence. Alexander Hamilton, the first Secretary of the Treasury, argued in 1781 that banks "have proved to be the happiest engines that were invented for advancing trade," but Professor Benjamin Klebaner has reminded us in his excellent history of commercial banking in the United States that Hamilton could point to no examples in this country, and very few elsewhere. To illustrate: in 1775 there was no bank worthy of the name in the colonies; in 1781, the first bank was organized in Philadelphia (in the same year incidentally that Cornwallis surrendered at Yorktown); and by 1800 some 28 banks in 12 states had been chartered, with offices in all of the major cities. In addition, Congress had chartered a bank in 1791, located in Philadelphia with branches operating in five states. In his history, Professor Klebaner noted that while Britain had five chartered banks by 1794, a full century after the establishment of the Bank of England, only 13 years after the establishment of the first U.S. bank there were 18 banks in the new United States. What explains this?

The principal explanation is, I think, obvious though rarely explored. The new nation faced a glittering prospect that never before had been encountered by another nation – namely, that a very large portion of the North American continent in which the United States was located lay open for development. Moreover, that portion began to grow rapidly. For example, President Thomas Jefferson's Louisiana Purchase in 1803 doubled the size of the new country, adding territory from the Mississippi River to the Rocky Mountains and from the Gulf of Mexico to British North America. Later additions, by purchase or treaty, continued to expand the nation. For example, two-fifths of Mexico was ceded to the U.S. at the conclusion of the war between the two countries. Not only did the U.S. possess an unusual number of restless, entrepreneurial types, seeking a better life than they had left behind ("behind" included, of course, the rocky soil of New England in addition to Britain and Europe), but also there existed dazzling opportunities for wealth, position (including political position) and power. The major problem was the ability to finance these opportunities and, to many, banking seemed to be the only answer. It was not at all surprising that the first bank chartered in the new nation was named "The Bank of North America" rather than for the city in which it opened (Philadelphia).

Virtually from the day banks first appeared in this country they conducted their loan business differently than English banks. In the United States there was, clearly, a pressing need for financing trade transactions. But equally important – in fact, a driving force in the development of U.S. banking – was the need for loans to build the new economy. Not surprisingly, U.S. commercial banks were also our first investment banking organizations.

In his towering study of early American banking, Professor Fritz Redlich of Harvard University described the pressure on banks to facilitate business transactions, but also to spur the development of capital resources. Country banks led the way in the late 1700s: "The lending of funds for the development of capital resources became the primary function of country banks, while the combination of lending on goods in transit with lending [for capital development] became the characteristic feature of city banking." Redlich noted that the latter loans were typically of two- or three-month duration, with payment accomplished at the end of that period. On the other hand, loans for capital development (often called "accommodation loans") were also for two- or three-month periods, but with the understanding that they would be renewed continually until the project – for example, machinery, ships or, literally, the creation of new towns and cities – had begun to produce revenue. Redlich pointed out that "in contrast to sound English commercial banking practices, permanent bank loans in this country became well-nigh universal in the [late 1700s] and so remained for decades to come."

Another feature of banking that made it particularly useful to entrepreneurs was the provision by banks of circulating medium to communities and the nation. Banknotes payable to bearers served as U.S. currency until 1863, when we had our first national currency – namely, national bank notes, backed by U.S. Treasury securities. The alternative was to rely solely on "hard money," such as gold and silver coin, of which debtor nations such as the United States had very little. Thus, the ability of banks to furnish a community, a city or a state with currency was often advanced as the reason for granting a bank charter, and in many cases turned out to be quite justified. But, on the other hand, whenever banks failed, leaving behind only worthless currency, the public's reaction was often a call to abolish the business of banking, with the degree of outrage suggesting that public hanging would not have been far behind. This was beginning to happen with some frequency by the 1830s.

The divisiveness of the banking issue even produced a serious problem for the drafters of the U.S. Constitution. Put simply, the Constitution said nothing about banking, most particularly a central bank chartered by Congress. Apparently the drafters assumed that any mention of the banking business, pro or con, would set off a furor that could threaten the acceptance of the Constitution itself. Even though the U.S. Supreme Court on several occasions subsequently made it clear that Congress did have the authority to charter a bank, and that state banks did have the authority to issue banknotes, these questions were never really settled until about the 1850s. For example, many years after the U.S. Supreme Court held that Congress could charter a bank, President Andrew Jackson stated in a message to Congress, at the beginning of his second term in 1833, that: "both the constitutionality and the expedience of the law creating this Bank are well questioned by a large portion of our fellow citizens," referring to the nation's first central bank, the Second Bank of the United States. The Constitution, therefore, left unresolved the question of how a central bank could fit into the legislative, judicial and executive structure established by the Constitution. Even today it is not unusual to hear the Federal Reserve described as the "fourth branch of government" by some of its partisans.

The appropriateness, legality and even constitutionality of banking were major issues in the years prior to the Civil War. Doing a banking business presented to political parties the same kind of political fault-line that slavery did later in the century or that abortion does in the early 21st century. Emotions ran high and political parties were often forced to support or oppose the very business of banking and, at the same time, try to hold their parties together. It was not easy.

What was there about banking that could compel the drafters of the Constitution to omit any reference to banks in that document, the absence of which provided the fuel for one of the great political and financial crises in the new nation? Or why was antagonism to banking so powerful that as late as 1852 the Secretary of the Treasury reported that in seven of the then 31 states, and in the three organized territories, there were no incorporated banks, in most cases because doing a banking business was prohibited by the state constitution?

The earliest problems came from the so-called agrarians, who simply regarded banking as an evil, designed to steal from the real producers of wealth – honest tillers of the soil, for example – the fruits of their labor. Bray Hammond in his Pulitzer Prize winning history *Banks and Politics in America* quotes one influential agrarian leader in Pennsylvania who, in reaction to the establishment of the first U.S. bank, the Bank of North America, in 1781, said:

> This institution, having no principle but that of avarice, which dries and shrivels up all of the manly, all the generous feelings of the human soul, will never be varied in its object and if continued will accomplish its end – to engross all the wealth, power and influence of the state.

Agrarianism tended to lose much of its force in the 19th century, but slowly, and it has never entirely disappeared. Although Thomas Jefferson recognized the usefulness of banks in certain circumstances, he was, I suspect, a "closet agrarian," while his major political rival, Alexander Hamilton, had precisely the opposite view.

As I pointed out earlier, a more difficult problem for banking was that of assuring a sound currency. A front-page editorial in an Ohio newspaper from the 1830s that I encountered while doing my doctorate research on early American banking illustrates the intensity of the problem. The issue was Ohio's plan to re-charter most of the banks then in existence in the state. The editor wrote:

> There is not a single bank in the United States that is much better than a den of thieves, seeking an opportunity to "fail" to advantage and rob the people! How disgusting, then, is the hypocritical jargon of the bank lackies and slaves about the recharter of the "good banks," "sound banks!" Pish! Humbug! – HOW CAN GOODNESS come out of HELL?

Currency problems, while serious, were not enough to account for the flames around the business of banking. After all, even early in our history, many cities and states had sound banks, some of which are still doing business today. Their banknotes circulated at par locally and in distant communities at a negligible discount, reflecting the cost of shipping currency to the issuing banks for redemption. Publications, usually weekly or monthly, known as "banknote reporters" were widely available and kept handy by every businessperson accepting currency. These publications listed every bank issuing currency, giving the discount, if any, to be applied. "No sale" generally meant that the bank had failed or was fictitious.

The most important problem facing banking was attributable to the existence of sound, well-established banks. Charters were difficult to obtain and generally available only from state legislatures. Persons who had an easy access to bank facilities – directors or large stockholders, for example – possessed an essential entrepreneurial tool in a new, growing economy. This tool was access to credit. Those who did not have such an advantage, or who believed they were frozen out because of their political affiliation or some other reason, attacked banking bitterly, at least until a turn of the political wheel brought new faces into a state's legislature. Politics in that day made those today seem tame.

The story of the chartering of the Manhattan Company in 1799, arranged by Aaron Burr, is described in fascinating detail in a biography of Alexander Hamilton by Ron Chernow. New York City had only one bank at the time. It was the Bank of New York, established in 1784 with the help of Alexander Hamilton and still in business today. The Bank of New York was often accused of favoring Federalists in its policies. At the time, Burr and Hamilton were not friends, but neither were they enemies. They were merely competing attorneys. Burr persuaded Hamilton that they should join forces in a new, bipartisan commission, consisting of Federalists and Republicans (the name at the time of Jefferson's party, to which Burr was devoted) for the purpose of bringing pure water to the city. He suggested that Hamilton be one of the members of the commission and, in fact, it was Hamilton who was most responsible for the success of the commission. The problem, however, was that Burr had not the slightest interest in using the charter to bring a new, improved water system to the city and, instead, was interested only in using the charter to create a new bank, which would compete with the Bank of New York. He had inserted provisions in the charter to make this possible and the new company "continued to draw impure water from old wells." The name of the new bank is a familiar one even today – the Chase Manhattan Bank.

Hamilton, needless to say, was furious. In a private letter he said that Burr "has lately by a trick established a <u>bank</u>, a perfect monster in its principles, but a very convenient instrument of <u>power and influence</u>." [Underscoring in original] Although Burr and Hamilton later clashed on numerous occasions, some on far more important issues than a bank charter, Hamilton clearly never forgot the way he had been tricked by Burr. The relationship between the two worsened over the years, to the extent that Burr challenged Hamilton to a duel at which Hamilton was killed in 1804.

There are so many illustrations of the intense warfare between supporters and opponents of banking that volumes would be needed to document that history. One incident, however, that I thought particularly interesting has been described in the superb recent biography of Abraham Lincoln by David Herbert Donald. In 1840, Illinois, along with most other states, had authorized its banks to refuse to redeem their notes in good funds (usually described in histories as the "suspension" of specie payments) because of the serious nationwide depression then underway. The Illinois legislature was controlled by generally anti-bank Democrats who had found a chink in the Illinois law that could be used to force the State Bank of Illinois to resume "specie payments" earlier than had been intended, which, of course, it could not do. The intention of the Democrats was to force the bank to fail, thereby reinforcing Democrat claims that losses taken by holders of the bank's currency were further proof of the evil of banking. The generally pro-bank Whigs in the legislature repeatedly prevented a quorum by walking out each time the issue arose. In one instance, however, the Whigs were unable to leave because the Democrats began to call the roll after barring the doors, whereupon a group of Whig legislators, led by Abraham Lincoln, jumped out of a second-story window of the state house. It was for naught. The Speaker recorded Lincoln and his friends as "present" and the Democrats thereafter took to referring to "Mr. Lincoln and his flying brethren." One newspaper went so far as to make the uncharitable comment that Lincoln could hardly be credited with taking a daring leap, because "his legs reached nearly from the window to the ground."

The Key Decade – 1830-40. With the benefit of time, we are now able to see that the foundation of today's banking system was put in place essentially between 1830 and 1840, notwithstanding the continuing warfare between "pro" and "anti" bank forces. In the decade of the 1830s, President Jackson set out to destroy the nation's first real central bank (the Second Bank of the United States, the forerunner of today's Federal Reserve). He believed that the Second Bank exerted excessive power over other banks and over the economy as a whole. The resulting "Bank War" of the 1830s, which is the way it is almost always described by historians, became one of the most important banking events in the nation's history, providing the trigger for fundamental development of its banking laws.

The battle is often characterized as a dramatic personal struggle between Andrew Jackson, the President of the United States, and Nicholas Biddle, the President of the Second Bank of the United States. Or it is also explained as a struggle between agrarians, farmers and working persons on the one hand versus bankers and important business interests on the other. Neither characterization, while not entirely groundless, is an adequate explanation. The real battle took place within the banking and financial industry. It was a battle between financial forces centered in Philadelphia and in certain southern states versus New York and Boston bankers and financiers. The Northeasterners thought that they were being constrained and restrained by the Second Bank from using to the full extent their banking powers and superior banking abilities to accomplish all kinds of projects. The Philadelphians and some Southerners attached considerable importance to stability, which was one of the primary objectives of any central bank.

The "Bank War" became one of the bitterest political battles that ever plagued the United States. In fact, it is not clear to this day whether President Jackson fully understood or agreed with the parties that so quickly fell in behind him and gave him the power to destroy the Second Bank. He did this by vetoing in 1832 an early attempt by Congress to extend the Second Bank's charter and then having the Secretary of the Treasury remove all federal funds from the Second Bank. And it is also possible that Nicholas Biddle, President of the Second Bank, never truly understood why he was suddenly regarded (and often referred to) as a "monster" or worse. Jackson's veto message was wildly popular, so that when the charter of the Second Bank expired in 1836, its only option was to become a state-chartered Pennsylvania bank. The United States was to be without a central bank for the next 77 years.

A good indication of the source of opposition to the Second Bank was provided by the fact that President Jackson's veto occurring when the charter still had four years to run led to a doubling in the number of banks in the country between 1832 and 1836. What accounted for this was anticipation of the freedom that would be possible for banks once the Second Bank was no longer the central bank. Even 77 years later, when the Federal Reserve was established, there was frequent mention of President Jackson's fear of a giant bank not really under any control except that of the President. Consequently, the 1913 Act creating the Federal Reserve System provided that there be 12 Federal Reserve Banks, not merely one.

As a direct outgrowth of the "Bank War," the strongly pro-Jackson New York state legislature in 1838 settled the question of who should have the right to obtain a bank charter with the enactment of its "Free Banking Act." The answer: everyone. The idea that any group of respectable citizens was entitled to apply for (and by implication receive) a bank charter soon swept through most other states, climaxing finally in the decision by the federal government in 1863 to adopt its own free banking act, which was titled the National Bank Act. Bray Hammond, not especially an admirer of "free banking," called it "the most important event in American banking history, [establishing] a distinctly American system of banking." In 1863, Congress had intended at the same time to put an end to all state-chartered banks by giving to national banks the exclusive right to issue a currency backed by Treasury securities. However, demand deposit banking was becoming popular so that the loss of the right to issue currency was not enough to close state banks. For example, a borrower from the bank could have his demand deposit account credited with the proceeds of the loan. Very shortly state-chartered banks again exceeded the number of national banks, giving us the "dual banking system," an arrangement that still exists, though one that is now thoroughly dominated by the federal government.

"Free banking" created a banking system and structure that was unique among nations. First, it nailed down the fact that banking would be done largely by private persons rather than by government, with the number of banks being determined primarily by market forces rather than government edict. Second, banking would be supervised and regulated by paid employees of government. This was a novel idea when it first appeared in New York in 1829 and was often strongly opposed because of a belief that governments should only be permitted to examine banks if they had, at the same time, an ownership interest in the banks examined. It is likely that the early introduction of paid government examiners accounts for the fact that supervision and regulation of banks in the United States has been more detailed and strict than in most other nations.

Because "free banking" provided virtually free entry into banking, it clearly brought with it an enhanced risk of bank failures, which in the 1830s had plagued banking. Most applicants for bank charters were reputable people, but not all were bright, experienced bankers. As one noted professor once put it years ago: The United States, to be sure, has 13,000 banks, but the problem is that it does not have 13,000 bankers. Accordingly, from the outset it was necessary to devise ways of protecting depositors (or holders of bank currency in early years) against any loss due to a bank failure. "Free banking" laws attempted to take care of one element of this by providing that currency issues must be backed by certain assets, such as state bonds or mortgages. After 1863, all currency was issued by national banks and backed by U.S. Treasury securities. (Today, of course, almost all U.S. currency is issued by Federal Reserve Banks).

Many people have assumed that the guarantee by government of bank deposits began with the establishment of the FDIC in 1933. In fact, it began more than a century earlier, in 1829, when New York State, then in the process of re-chartering most of its banks, established a "safety fund" to be used to pay note holders of failed banks and, for at least the first few years, a failed bank's depositors as well. Most of the early state plans focused on currency safety, but after checkable bank deposits began to replace banknotes as the major portion of the circulating medium, eight states provided deposit guarantee plans, although not very successfully. It is not often realized that the United States – and only the United States – had an unbroken, century-long history of state and federal efforts to protect banknote holders and depositors of failed banks, well before the creation of the FDIC.

My intention in this chapter has been to explain why a banking system that seemed to have been put together so haphazardly has been able to survive – on occasion to become even more complex. The answer is that the system was based on a wide and strong consensus on two basic principles, almost as powerful today as they were almost 200 years ago. These principles can be expressed in terms of objectives or fears, with the latter possibly more meaningful in this instance: First, there was fear of a concentration of banking power in private or government hands. Second, there was a fear of banking instability and bank failures, which bore particularly heavily on unsophisticated bank depositors or other creditors with small balances. Failure to deal with this problem presented a strong risk of political disaster for the banking structure.

In a number of instances, several of which I will describe later, whenever a difficult banking system problem had to be resolved, the action taken was consistent with one or both of these principles. I don't mean to imply that a different set of guiding principles would not have been better. It is simply a fact that the present banking system was created purposefully, with both of these objectives clearly in mind. Today's banking system was not an accident.

Section I
Government Years

I suppose that few persons forget their first real job. This was certainly true in my case. Following several years of accepting short-term teaching contracts at various New York colleges while completing my doctorate studies at Columbia University, I applied for a position at the Federal Deposit Insurance Corporation as a financial economist, and was accepted. Not surprisingly, therefore, the four chapters in Section I deal with the impressions I received and several events I witnessed at the Corporation during the nine years I was there.

Chapter One describes the FDIC in 1951, focusing on the activities in which it was engaged, but also includes commentary on the political climate in the 1950s. The other three chapters deal with policies developed by the FDIC intended to assure that the agency, born in the early 1930s, would not suffer the same fate that most of the state-sponsored deposit insurance systems had met. There were, in fact, several remarkably successful early state systems, but the large majority failed after encountering a severe economic depression. At least one of the chapters in this Section (Chapter Four) may come as a surprise to persons who are familiar with the FDIC's history, but are not aware of the significant contribution made by its leading economist, Dr. Clark Warburton.

Chapter One
The Beginning of My Journey

If, by 1951, I had settled firmly on fashioning a career somewhere in banking, I could not have done better than begin by seeking employment with the Federal Deposit Insurance Corporation. The Corporation was one of the new federal agencies created at the outset of the Roosevelt Administration in 1933. No other institution, public or private, had so sweeping a mandate or so extensive a writ when it came to the banking system. The FDIC was charged with nothing less than restoring to bank depositors the losses (up to a specific ceiling amount) they had suffered because of a bank failure. Virtually all commercial banks in the U.S. participated in this program. Also included were a number of mutual savings banks, but most institutions that were special-purpose lenders, such as savings and loan associations, were included in a different federal system.

The deposit insurance provisions were part of the Banking Act of 1933 and were credited by many persons for the Act's successful enactment, which had many controversial sections. The deposit insurance sections were also controversial but, at the same time, were immensely popular except among the very largest banks, which feared that they would wind up paying the bill. The Administration was divided, with President Franklin D. Roosevelt opposing the insurance proposal, ostensibly because of its anticipated cost. Probably more important, however, was a fear, particularly of some of the President's close advisors, that once established, deposit insurance would make it difficult to bring about sweeping changes in the banking structure. And so it turned out.

Within the banking industry itself, support of the deposit insurance proposal was deep and powerful because of the overwhelming support from smaller banks. There is no question that their intensive lobbying played a significant part in bringing about passage of the legislation. These banks constituted, by number, the large majority of all banks in the country. They regarded deposit insurance as essential to their survival and were determined that there be no fundamental change in the U.S. banking structure.

The popularity of deposit insurance among the general public was easy to understand. The FDIC opened for business at the beginning of January 1934. During the four preceding years there had been more than 9,000 bank failures, between 80 and 90 percent of which were small, state-chartered banks. Early in the depression, many state governors had begun to declare banking "holidays," allowing banks to close temporarily, or to do a highly restricted business. Then, on March 5, 1933, the newly inaugurated President Roosevelt declared a national banking holiday that lasted 14 days, after which the panic stemming from widespread bank failures subsided. Still, many of the banks that closed during those 14 days never reopened.

The FDIC was 16 years old in 1950 when I was at Columbia University finishing research on my doctoral thesis dealing with early western banking in the United States. I knew very little about the Corporation except for a general awareness of its function. My application for a job was not part of a well-thought-out career strategy, but more closely resembled an act of desperation. Teaching positions were scarce in 1950, at least among economic historians, but a close friend had heard that the FDIC had been searching for some time for an individual to add to its research staff who had studied early U.S. banking. He suggested giving that agency a call.

As it turned out, from the day that it had been created in 1933, the FDIC had been collecting material on the operations of the 14 state deposit guarantee plans that had operated at various times between 1829 and 1930. A few had been exceptionally successful, but most found it impossible to continue for very long. My doctoral thesis dealt in some detail with two of the most successful guarantee plans – those of Indiana and Ohio prior to the Civil War – along with the reasons for the spectacular failure of Michigan's plan by 1840. I applied to the FDIC, mentioning the foregoing, was quickly accepted, and reported for work in 1951 as a financial economist.

My first, and continuing, assignment was to take responsibility for assembling and, where necessary, editing or writing portions of the FDIC's Annual Report to the President of the Senate and to the Speaker of the House of Representatives. At the time this was the only publication by the FDIC that received wide distribution, primarily because it was an important source book, heavily statistical in content and covering all commercial banks.

My assignment was received with relief by the only other economist then on the FDIC's research staff, Dr. Clark Warburton. He was engaged in far more important work and was delighted to pass this particular responsibility on to someone else, although he did assist considerably in the transition and always kept a wary eye on me in subsequent years. On the other hand, I was immensely grateful for the assignment, not only because it meant that I would be working with an outstanding economist, but also because I could obtain a valuable education in the intricacies of the complex U.S. banking system and structure, a subject about which, in 1951, I was close to being totally ignorant.

A Political Hitch. This should be the end of my story of employment by the FDIC, except for an unexpected event that had the effect of altering my position in that Corporation.

The Korean War had begun in June 1950, and by 1951 when I joined the FDIC, there was a great effort underway by government agencies to speed the recruitment of economists because of an anticipation of the reappearance of the World War II programs involving price controls, rationing and other such matters. My application had been caught up in this wave, even though my particular skill was not one that facilitators had in mind. I was told by the FDIC to report to work immediately, although several of the required letters from former colleagues on my supposed abilities had not been received. One such letter did arrive about a month later, praising my speaking and writing abilities, at least as my former colleague saw them. Unfortunately, the letter ended with the writer's strong insistence that he knew whereof he spoke because he and I had worked together closely for several years in the Young Republican Club of Rockland County, N.Y. As I quickly found out, the rule followed by the FDIC (and I assume by other so-called "independent" federal agencies) was that no new employee above a clerical level could be hired without the approval of the Chairman of the Democrat Party in the county from which the applicant had come. I might note that Washington in the early 1950s, particularly under President Harry S Truman, was a distinctly southern city with personnel policies dictated by senior Congressional Democrats from the South. These Congressmen held the senior positions and worked closely with Democrat "machines" in the north, such as those in New York, Chicago and Kansas City. The objective of the southern Democrats was to keep Washington a quintessential southern city in all respects, which meant that for more than a few northerners, in the 1950s Washington was not a particularly comfortable city in which to live or work.

The Chairman of the FDIC at the time, Maple T. Harl, was a fervent supporter of the kind of Kansas City politics that had generated the "no Republican need apply" rule, but he had been ill and was not expected to return for about a month. This gave the FDIC's Director of Personnel and the Chief of the Research Division an opportunity to slip my application through without attracting special attention. In about three weeks the chief of my division met me in the hall and, in a low voice, said: "Unpack – you are staying."

What made all of this important for me was that, a year or so later, Gen. Dwight D. Eisenhower was elected President. The new President was a product of one of the largest bureaucracies in Washington (the U.S. Army) and did not share the view of most Republicans in 1952, namely that the Washington bureaucracy consisted largely of leftwing New Dealers, if not worse. As Theodore H. White, the well-known chronicler of Presidents (and not a particular fan of President Eisenhower at the outset), put it in one of his final books: "It is not demeaning Eisenhower to say that he was not only a great commander and a great President, but a great bureaucrat . . . He knew how to use government, and how government worked." Mr. Eisenhower was the only President of whom I am aware who immediately after his election held a reception for all senior-level federal civil service employees in Washington, with no assumption that political party affiliations had any relevancy. Although I missed his invitation cut by one grade level, I was assured by several people from the FDIC who had attended that the President personally shook hands with every individual there, notwithstanding a very long receiving line. Later, I was to see a vivid example of the President's approach to management while working in the Senate on temporary detail from the FDIC.

President Eisenhower's attitude toward federal employees was not at all the same as that of Republicans flooding into Washington after a 20-year exile. Many of these Republicans were suspicious of all employees even though, so far as I could see, FDIC employees divided essentially along the same political lines as did the country. On the other hand, there was some reason for those taking over management of the FDIC to be concerned because a small group of senior FDIC personnel refused to give up their offices, contending that their positions were protected by Civil Service rules. This was a complete departure from the past position of the FDIC, which as an independent agency had always considered itself exempt from many of these rules. My recollection is that the Republicans stationed armed guards in the corridors to refuse entry by the former occupants of offices. This led to a legal action of some sort against the Corporation. It did not receive a great deal of publicity, and I do not recall how it was resolved (except that the old officials disappeared). In addition, I have the impression that there was a settlement that left the FDIC, at least for the time I was there, free from many of the Civil Service rules that were followed by cabinet agencies such as Agriculture, Treasury and Interior.

Of course, when the changeover occurred I was in a charmed position because for more than a year, as a result of the employment flap I described,

I had been accepted as one of those rare creatures – an admitted Republican. With the change in Administration, I quickly found myself writing some of the speeches for the new (now Republican) Chairman, Henry E. Cook, or working on pieces of testimony or analyzing proposed legislation. In effect, while remaining in the Division of Research, and continuing my annual report assignment, I began to work more closely with the General Counsel's Office. By the time I left the FDIC, in early 1960, I was spending most of my time doing legislative and public policy work, an interest that has continued to the present day. During that tenure, I had served under two other FDIC Chairmen in addition to Harl and Cook. They were Ray M. Gidney, who was Acting Chairman briefly in 1957 and Jesse P. Wolcott, who served from then into the early 1960s.

This bit of personal history completed, it is time to return to the subject of this and the following chapter: the significant contributions made by the FDIC to shaping the evolving banking system during the several decades that followed the end of World War II. This is not a story well-known to the outside world. Indeed, it was not widely recognized at the time even within much of the FDIC. For one thing, histories of the FDIC tend to focus almost exclusively on the Corporation's experience in dealing with bank failures or banking crises. Periods such as the 1950s and 1960s were, therefore, passed over rather quickly since there were virtually no bank failures and banking crises were little more than a distant memory. The real story could be found only by looking beyond (or more accurately, behind) what was happening. The fact is that the work done by the FDIC during the "quiet decades," from the 1940s through the 1960s, very possibly exceeded in importance anything that happened before or since in the Corporation's 75-year history. But first, it is worth taking a quick look at the FDIC as it appeared when I joined it.

FDIC in the 1950s. In 1951, the FDIC was a very small government agency. It occupied only three and a half floors of a large, downtown office building, plus a small-attached building soon to be demolished. A visitor arriving in Washington by train or plane who directed the cab driver to be taken to the Federal Deposit Insurance Corporation was likely to be met with a blank stare, unless remembering to add: "the National Press Building at the corner of 14th and F." The number of employees was barely over 1,000 in 1951, and only about 300 were located in Washington, the remainder being distributed among 12 regional offices. At the end of the decade, in 1960, the FDIC was still occupying leased office space in the National Press Building at the corner of 14th and F Streets and had increased in size only by 200 employees, most of whom had joined as additional bank examiners and were stationed in the regional offices. By the end of the next decade (in 1970) total employment was pushing 2,500, again primarily because of growth in the Division of Bank Supervision. Moreover, it was also beginning to reflect the transformation of the FDIC into a "federal banking agency" with a variety of additional responsibilities that had little to do with the deposit insurance function.

Although one might be entitled to assume that the FDIC's initials pretty much told what business it was in, this was hardly the case in 1951 or, for that matter, for almost any time in the Corporation's 75-year history. In fact, during the period on which I am now focusing – the 1950s and 1960s– the business done by the FDIC was examining state-chartered banks that were not members of the Federal Reserve System (in number, more than half of all commercial banks holding insured deposits) along with about 200 mutual savings banks, which were concentrated mainly in New England. To this was added the necessary tracking of the work of other state and federal banking agencies with respect to the deposit insurance interests of the FDIC. All of which explains why, during the several decades following the end of World War II, 70 to 80 percent of all FDIC employees were in the Division of Examination and why, by the 1950s, the primary "business" of the new agency was supervising and regulating banks. It is only when one looks at the FDIC as a regulatory or supervisory agency rather than as an insurance company, and most particularly as a bank examining agency, that it becomes clear that the Corporation's contributions to a new and much strengthened banking system were significant.

As for management, the FDIC was run by a board of directors, consisting of two directors appointed by the President and the Comptroller of the Currency. By law, the directors had to be from different political parties. The Comptroller, who also was appointed by the President, served as the third member of the FDIC Board in an *ex officio* capacity. Fortunately for the FDIC, the Corporation at that time was run mostly by the professional individuals who had come together 15 or 16 years earlier to staff the FDIC office. Able persons were numerous and available in the depths of the depression, and whoever did the original FDIC staffing took full advantage of the opportunity. I know I was quite impressed when I arrived in 1951 when most of those "founding" persons were still in place.

The fact is that the real direction of the FDIC during the post-World War II decades came not from the directors, but from the division chiefs, particularly the Chief of the Division of Examination, who had reporting to him something like 80 percent or more of all employees at the Corporation. The division heads, including the Chief of the Division of Research and Statistics, were also unusually competent individuals so that the FDIC encountered no serious management problems in the 1950s and 1960s.

An incident involving the preparation of a piece of testimony for one of the chairmen is illustrative. At the time, all public speeches or testimony by a chairman or director were read aloud to the "Reading Committee," consisting of senior representatives from each division of the Corporation (about seven or eight persons), for possible corrections and final approval. I was the author of numerous pieces during my time at the FDIC and on this occasion was presenting testimony favoring a piece of proposed legislation in which I had included a paragraph stating that the Corporation had strongly supported similar legislation in the past. The Committee immediately said that this paragraph had to be deleted and, notwithstanding my protestations, gave no reasons. As it happened, a 10-minute recess was called at that moment and while I sat waiting for the members of the Committee to return, one of the members came over to me quite privately and said: "Carter, when the Chairman of this agency ties his shoelaces in the morning, he has completed the greatest mental effort of which he is capable. Including that paragraph would offer an opportunity for one of the Congressmen to ask the Chairman to elaborate on the current position of the Corporation, which the Chairman would not be able to do. So stop arguing and cut the paragraph." I did.

So far as the finances of the FDIC were concerned, the procedure devised was rather straightforward and presented no special problems. In 1935, Dr. Clark Warburton of the FDIC's Division of Research had been asked to examine the record of bank failures during the prior 70 years, including depositor losses, and to suggest an annual assessment rate that likely would be sufficient in the future. He concluded that one-twelfth of one percent of domestic deposits would do the trick, except in periods when the economy was in deep depression. The FDIC was agreeable, but only if it were given the power to examine the roughly 60 percent of the banking industry, in terms of the number of banks, that was poorly supervised (if at all) by the states (except for a very small number of states, such as New York). This was agreed to, and shortly after the adoption of the 1933 legislation this examination power was provided. Nevertheless, the FDIC continued to point out that even with the new examination power, the assessments would not be sufficient to cover losses to depositors of the magnitude that occurred during the depression years of the 1870s, the 1890s and, of course, the early 1930s. This plan, which eventually made provision for assessment credits to the banks in years of low FDIC losses, could have continued up to the present day. However, a changed system, focusing on the size of the "deposit insurance fund" (i.e., the Corporation's net worth) was put in its place, following the banking crisis of the late 1980s and early 1990s. This system was no particular improvement and, more probably, was a mistake.

At this juncture, it may be appropriate to add a few comments on the use of the word "insurance," which has long puzzled many persons and also may leave readers wondering. Until the establishment of the FDIC, proposals for protecting depositors in failed banks were known generally as "deposit guarantee" systems. However, all of the state systems that had been established during the early decades of the 20th century had failed or closed by 1930, so that the idea of "deposit guarantee" was considered bad odor in Washington, even among community bankers who in 1933 desperately needed some kind of government guarantee of deposits. As one excellent account of the deliberations in the Congress over the new legislation put it, "the mere mention of deposit guarantees could induce a banker 'to show every sign of incipient apoplexy.'" In short, deposit guarantee was regarded as a radical but failed method of protecting depositors. It is not surprising therefore, that proponents of the 1933 legislation took special pains to insist that the depositor protection provisions of the Banking Act of 1933 did not constitute a government guarantee of deposits but was, rather, an "insurance" plan.

It was not insurance by any stretch of the imagination, nor is it insurance today, as the term is commonly understood. To be sure, the legislation was dressed up with terms that are associated with an ordinary insurance company, such as "deposit insurance premiums" or the "deposit insurance fund." The latter – the FDIC's "surplus" now goes under the grand name of "deposit insurance fund" – offers a good illustration of the problem. Each year, the net income of the FDIC, after deducting insurance expenditures and operating costs, is turned over to the U.S. Treasury, which utilizes these receipts in the same way that it would utilize any other tax receipts – namely, by paying government bills. But to keep the illusion alive, the Treasury Department gives to the Corporation securities equal to the amount turned over to it by the FDIC. In this instance the FDIC has no options; all funds over and above operating costs and insurance expenses must be turned over to the Treasury, and the Treasury must give some indication that it has received these funds. In Damon Runyon's day, the securities turned over to the FDIC would be more appropriately called "markers," since all they did was keep track of how much receipts have exceeded expenditures (or vice versa). For when these Treasury securities are actually used, they must be sold to the public causing an increase in the federal debt. In an excellent study of the difficulties faced by the FDIC in recent years (1988 to 1991), David S. Holland works his way through the confusing verbiage of official reports and then reminds readers "After all, stripped to its fundamentals, deposit insurance was, and is, no more than a government guarantee of the repayment of deposits, up to a certain amount, in a failed bank."

Most confusing of all was the inevitable use of the term "insured bank." There is, of course, no such animal; banks never have been, nor are they today, "insured" by the FDIC. It is the depositors who are insured. The correct designation would be "banks holding deposits insured by the FDIC," but most persons avoid it (and I am one of the culprits). Unfortunately, therefore, there are some who tend to look at deposit insurance as a product produced by the government and sold to banks, which gives rise to fascinating articles by academics on the pricing of deposit insurance, and tempts bankers to believe that, given the absence of any capital stock, bankers have some sort of financial stake in the deposit insurance fund (i.e. surplus) of "their" corporation.

Perhaps the most telling indictment of the "insurance" camouflage was provided by the General Accounting Office (GAO), a prestigious federal agency, but one not particularly noted for its expertise when dealing with banking. In 1991 the GAO, the auditing arm of Congress, suddenly declared that the FDIC's "deposit insurance fund" was a negative $7 billion. The Chairman of the FDIC, L. William Seidman, characterized this conclusion as "magic accounting," with the GAO "merely playing with the numbers." He was correct, of course, for if anyone had really believed that the so-called "deposit insurance fund" had disappeared, there would have been panic in the streets. However, the only people who seemed to believe it were a few bankers and academics. The general public ignored the entire thing in magnificent fashion, recognizing that it was the federal government that was guaranteeing the payment of "insured" deposits to depositors in failed banks. Accordingly, the public paid no attention to the games being played with the "size" of the "deposit insurance fund," or the problem of its "restoration."

Missions of the FDIC. "Mission" is a word with a wide variety of meanings. My unabridged Random House Dictionary contains no fewer than 20 definitions, most of them reflecting a religious or government foreign affairs background. Here I am using, as it happens, the 16th of the Random House offerings – namely, "an assigned duty or task." This is the usage commonly found in corporate planning documents, bank and non-bank.

For the FDIC, there was no question about the duty that had been assigned to it by the U.S. Congress. The Corporation's very first annual report began with a mission statement, a practice usually, but not always, followed in succeeding annual reports. For example, the annual report for 1947 stated: "the FDIC was created to protect bank depositors from losses arising out of bank failures." I used the 1947 statement, which was virtually identical to many of the others at the time, because it avoided the troublesome word "insurance" – as in "to insure depositors against loss" – a usage that was already beginning to be misunderstood. The only deviation from the flat mission statement found in most of the earlier annual reports was the addition of another sentence or two pointing out that by restoring deposits the Corporation was contributing to maintaining confidence in the banking system or making its contribution to the nation's financial stability.

Interestingly, in identifying bank depositors and other creditors as the principal beneficiaries of the guarantee, the FDIC's statement was similar to that made by the New York State legislature when it adopted the nation's first deposit guarantee plan in 1829, more than a century before the U.S. government got around to it:

> The loss by the insolvency of banks falls generally upon the farmer, the mechanic and the laborer who are least acquainted with the condition of banks and who, of all others, are [least able] to either guard against or to sustain a loss by their failure. The protection and security of this valuable portion of our population demands, from us, in their favor, our most untiring exertions . . .

There was also an interesting similarity in the way that the New York legislature and, many years later, the U.S. Congress identified the persons who most needed the protection of a guarantee plan. Banks in 1830 typically used their own banknotes when making loans, and those notes then circulated as currency. Of course, these immediately became worthless if the bank failed. Deposit banking was not very common, although it was becoming so in cities such as New York and Philadelphia. In any event, the New York plan protected depositors, but was primarily intended to protect persons holding a failed bank's currency. A century later, the U.S. Congress made it clear that it was the "rent and grocery" money of depositors that was uppermost in its mind by limiting coverage to $2,500 per depositor. This ceiling was quickly raised to $5,000 for each depositor, remaining so until 1949, when coverage was raised to $10,000, remaining at that level through 1965. Thus, the New York legislature in 1829 and the U.S. Congress in 1933 took quite different ways of reaching the same conclusion – namely, that the most important people to be protected were, in 1829, those who were left with currency in their hands that had suddenly lost its value or, in 1933, with a small deposit balance in a bank that was likely to have disappeared. What the later FDIC coverage limit of $100,000 (or $250,000) is intended to accomplish is no longer very clear.

The FDIC was given a second mission in 1933 by the Congress, closely related to the first, but fated to create controversy at a much later time, such as today. In 1933, the proponents of deposit insurance were seeking something more than reimbursement of depositors of failed banks, important as that might be. The FDIC was expected to use its powers to preserve and, if at all possible, to strengthen the existing banking system, i.e., one dominated (in terms of number of institutions) by community banks, holding a rather small share of total bank assets, but exercising much more political power than was suggested by their total assets. For many of the architects of the new program, the preservation and expansion of the banking structure in place was at least as important, if not of even greater importance, than the restoration of deposits in failed banks. And the FDIC indeed found ways, such as refusing to consider the absorption of exchange charges by correspondent banks as "interest on demand deposits." Paying interest on demand deposits was, of course, unlawful under the Banking Act of 1933. This gave to non-member state banks a competitive advantage when competing for correspondent balances, since the Federal Reserve was determined to wipe out "non-par" banking and prohibited the practice by its member banks, both national and state. [Non-par banking was the practice, long since outlawed, of a bank assessing an exchange charge for collecting checks. Only state non-member banks could do this and then only in a few states – Minnesota, North and South Dakota, and Montana, among others. If you banked in rural Minnesota, for example, and wrote a check to a store in Minneapolis, your hometown bank would "clip" the check when it was presented for collection, in effect making a small charge for paying the check. As you might understand, merchants weren't anxious to accept out-of town checks in non-par states.]

A federal guarantee of deposits had been the lifelong goal of the Chairman of the House Banking Committee in 1933, Rep. Henry B. Steagall (D-Ala.). At one point in the Congressional debate, when the support of community bankers was wavering because of rumors that the new agency might discriminate against small state banks, Steagall declared flatly: "No man is more concerned about preserving the independent community banks in the United States than I am . . . This bill will preserve independent, dual banking in the United States. This is what this bill is intended to do." At the time that he made this statement, the word "independent" generally meant banks with no branches, and "dual banking" almost certainly meant federal and state bank chartering, since one of the proposals by opponents of deposit insurance was to eliminate all state-chartered banks.

Another significant supporter of deposit insurance was Sen. Arthur H. Vandenberg (R-Mich.), whose last-minute amendment established a temporary insurance fund as of January 1, 1934. Otherwise, the permanent plan, which never in fact was adopted, would not take effect until July 1, 1934 (later extended to 1935). By providing for a temporary deposit insurance fund that would begin business on January 1, 1934, Vandenberg was seeking to forestall the possibility that opponents in the Roosevelt Administration might be able to defer, and later kill, implementation of the deposit insurance provisions of the Banking Act of 1933. The Senator quoted with approval editorial comment on his temporary plan, which was a part of the Senate bill then being reconciled in a House-Senate conference, from which deposit insurance advocates feared it might never emerge. As Vandenberg put it: "Foreshadowed was an America without small banks, an America whose credit would be controlled by a few men pulling the strings from New York . . . The Senate and House, by passing bank deposit guaranty bills, have taken the first government action of this Depression to reverse the vicious trend and save small banks."

One of the great fears of the small banks was the threat that acceptance of deposit insurance would require joining the Federal Reserve System, a prospect that these banks utterly opposed. In fact, there was just such a requirement in the Banking Act of 1933, scheduled to take effect at a later date. Loss of small bank support would threaten the entire Banking Act of 1933, but the issue was handled in an adroit manner by a member of the Conference Committee who at one meeting told the lawmakers with small bank constituencies: "There is nothing in the bill, not one thing, that should by itself cause any member to vote against the conference report. There will be other Congresses." Sure enough, the effective date of the Federal Reserve membership requirement was first postponed, and later quietly dropped.

In today's world, the two missions of the FDIC – to guarantee deposits in bank failures and to strengthen the banking system dominated by community banks – no longer have the kind of influence that was clear in the first three or four decades of deposit insurance. One reason is that the FDIC has changed. Whereas it was once an agency highly focused on its insurance function, it has become what we now call a "federal banking agency." This means that the FDIC, like the other federal agencies dealing with banks, has received a large number of new responsibilities, most of which in the case of the FDIC have no relevance at all to its basic objective, which is simply to restore deposits in failing banks. For example, enforcement of antitrust issues arising out of bank mergers or acquisitions by banks subject to FDIC supervision, or the many complex pieces of consumer legislation, means that the FDIC has become involved with things that have little to do with paying insured deposits of failed banks. One result is that the Corporation in the early 21st century is about six times larger than it was in the 1950s and 1960s, even though it has far fewer banks to examine than it had in those years. Today it is not the same agency to which I reported in 1951.

The FDIC has long been seeking another, or broader, mission. Insurance coverage of $100,000 per depositor [to say nothing of the increase to $250,000 during the 2008 financial crisis] is clearly excessive for achieving the first mission. Using the standards of the original legislation, one could protect the rent and grocery money of virtually every depositor with a coverage ceiling of about $50,000 per depositor or even less. There is only one reason for having individual coverage at $100,000 per depositor, or even higher [like the $250,000 limit set in 2008], and that is to achieve the second mission – namely, to preserve the existing banking structure. However, it is not politic to say this, so that the FDIC is left in a quandary: its first mission has been more than accomplished and its second mission is only partially attained by current coverage, but to go much further arouses intense opposition from those who see a serious "moral hazard" problem, (i.e., the temptation to make riskier loans because of the insurance protection). There are, of course, ways of dealing with this problem not covered here. At this point, I think the story of how the FDIC assured its own survival, particularly during the several decades following World War II, is a more interesting and important story—one that is now generally not known. Nonetheless, it still has important implications for the future.

Chapter Two
Creating an Effective "Lender of Last Resort"

When I arrived at the FDIC in early 1951, the Corporation was enjoying what appeared to be a quiet period. Bank failures were remarkably few in number, averaging three or four a year during the several decades following the end of World War II, and involved very small banks. The FDIC had been in business for about 17 years and had come through its opening years in the early 1930s with surprisingly few problems. When the war ended in 1945, and the widely expected postwar depression then failed to materialize, any problems facing the Corporation seemed to be minor.

Frankly, as a newcomer, I did not fully understand or appreciate the strong undercurrents shaping the FDIC's strategies during the immediate post-war decades. There were plenty of other things going on in banking that held one's attention, such as the campaign by Comptroller of the Currency James J. Saxon in the 1960s to expand the powers of national banks, and the bitter infighting between the Comptroller and the Federal Reserve which his campaign generated. Only later did I begin to understand just why the FDIC had encountered few problems during its earliest years and, more importantly, why it would make its most important contribution to the continued life of deposit insurance during the quiet decades that followed the end of World War II. It may be useful to begin by taking a quick look back at the 1930s.

FDIC in the 1930s. When the FDIC opened for business in 1934, the prospect of survival must have seemed grim. The banking disasters of the early 1930s had peaked on March 5, 1933, when President Roosevelt was compelled to declare a nationwide Bank Holiday, effectively closing every bank in the country. It was only after the banks reopened several weeks later that final work began on legislation creating the FDIC. That legislation, which was included in the Banking Act of 1933, was enacted on June 16, 1933. Soon thereafter, the Corporation was handed responsibility for regularly examining the (then) more than 7,000 banks that had been chartered by

17

the states, but which had not opted for membership in the Federal Reserve System. These banks had received little in the way of realistic supervision (except in a very few instances, such as in New York State) and accounted for almost all (probably 80 percent or more) of the bank failures during the four crisis years beginning with 1930.

Some of the first stories I heard at the FDIC in 1951 came from persons who in 1934-35 had been FDIC claim agents, responsible for paying depositors of failed banks. The objective had been to do this as quickly as possible so as to restore spending money to the stricken communities. The claim agents in those early years had braced themselves to deal with crowds of people vociferously demanding their money, but instead often found themselves staring at empty bank lobbies. Much of their time, I was told, was taken up telephoning depositors urging them to come in and pick up their deposits. The explanation seemed simple: payment of deposits of failed banks was handled in the first 20 or so cases through the immediate establishment of a Deposit Insurance National Bank, which generally occupied quarters in the failed bank. Depositors, therefore, recognized that their funds were safe and found no reason to rush to withdraw them. Of course, what this really reflected was that the very establishment of the FDIC had already gone some way toward restoring confidence in the banking system.

A new banking world began to emerge after the panic year of 1933. For example, President Roosevelt seemed quite willing to consider any reasonable move that might help end the Great Depression. During his campaign for the Presidency, Mr. Roosevelt had advocated such experimentation, saying in one speech:

> The country needs and, unless I mistake its temper, the country demands bold, persistent experimentation. It is common sense to take a method and try it. If it fails, admit it frankly and try another. But above all, try something.

A fiscal conservative, Mr. Roosevelt believed there was only a slight chance that federal deposit insurance would succeed. He, therefore, opposed the legislation, reportedly preferring to wait a bit before undertaking a thorough reorganization of the banking structure and system. But once established, the FDIC met the President's test: it immediately began to work. Little objection to the FDIC was heard from Mr. Roosevelt thereafter.

The FDIC in its initial years found an economy largely free of the panic mood that had been present in the early months of 1933. As a result, its task after opening in 1934 was largely to mop up the debris left over from the

Great Crash. Bank failures continued, of course, but not in such numbers or sizes as to give the FDIC any serious problems, although a few failures were rather large for the time. To be sure, cynics liked to remind Congress that the FDIC profited from the cleansing effect of the earlier years, which is to say that by the end of 1933 there were many fewer unsound banks left to fail. The critics would quickly add that this was only temporary.

In fact, a number of things contributed to a slow but clear restoration of confidence in the banking system in the early 1930s, though in my view the presence of the FDIC was the key. The attitude of the President also was quite important. For example, in his first fireside chat to the nation, he dealt with the matter of the Bank Holiday, virtually promising that when it ended only sound banks would be able to resume business. Since well over 3,000 of the banks closed during the Bank Holiday never reopened, this alone, in an interesting but perverse fashion, contributed to increasing public confidence in the banking system.

The FDIC received other important assistance as it began its formidable task in 1934. An important piece of assistance had been provided by President Hoover, who had sought desperately for the Federal Reserve's help in bringing an end to the wave of bank failures. But the Federal Reserve offered little or no assistance and, apparently, Mr. Hoover did not believe he had the authority to demand it. As I mentioned earlier, late in his Administration Mr. Hoover asked Congress to create the Reconstruction Finance Corporation, initially for the purpose of making loans to banking institutions to keep them from failing or for resurrecting them if they had already failed. For various reasons, including some important political problems, the RFC was not able to stem the avalanche of bank failures with its loans. But that agency proved of great help in making capital investments in banks once the crisis subsided. For example, it purchased the capital issues of 6,139 banks and invested more than $1 billion in bank capital, about one-third of the total capital in all banks in 1933. Perhaps the single most important change in the post-Bank Holiday years was the diminished influence of the Federal Reserve. The failure of the Fed to use its monetary powers to halt the economic decline that began in 1929 is now regarded, just about unanimously by economists, as the reason why the United States, rather than suffering a moderate recession in 1929, had to endure the worst financial calamity in its history – a severely depressed economy that lasted about 11 years, ending only with the onset of World War II. In fact, more than 17 percent of the U.S. labor force was still unemployed in 1939.

From the viewpoint of the FDIC, the critical failure of the Federal Reserve was not its monetary policy, as damaging as that turned out to be, but the Fed's refusal to address the bank failure problem. In 1877, Walter

Bagehot offered in *Lombard Street* his classic advice to central bankers facing a severe banking crisis – lend to sound banks as fulsomely as possible, but at high rates. However, the Federal Reserve, to the astonishment of many, took precisely the opposite course during the banking crisis of the 1930s. As Professor Allan H. Meltzer of Carnegie University put it in his recent, magnificent history of the Federal Reserve: "Nothing in theory or sensible banking practices can explain why the Federal Reserve did not respond to the failure of thousands of banks. Most of the banking failures from 1929 to 1932 and the final collapse in the winter of 1933 could have been avoided."

In 1932-33, it seems likely that essentially the same view of the Federal Reserve's duty was held by President Hoover and by President Roosevelt as well. Neither President did anything, however. The difficulty was that while Mr. Roosevelt had been elected President in November 1932, he would not be inaugurated until March 1933 (under the old system, since repealed). Mr. Hoover did not want to take action until consulting with, or acting jointly with, the new President. But Mr. Roosevelt refused to bind himself to anything until he had been sworn in. What forceful joint action taken by the two men during the approximately five months between the election and the inauguration would have accomplished is something that will never be known. Professor Meltzer, in his history, made the final, blunt assessment of the outcome: "The Federal Reserve had been indecisive and incompetent as the banking problem became a crisis. The Board now took a back seat. The Treasury and the new President made the policy decisions."

FDIC's "Third Mission." Earlier, in Chapter One, I had said that the FDIC had been given two closely related missions: to restore deposits in failed banks to each depositor, up to the statutory maximum, and to use every opportunity to strengthen the existing banking structure, the principal feature of which was the extraordinarily large number of banks. But from the moment the FDIC was created, a third, seldom-mentioned, mission emerged that was superior to the first two – a mission that would live for about 20 or 30 years before the perceived need for it disappeared. That "silent mission" was to preserve, at all costs, the solvency of the Corporation. This meant, among other things, giving the continued existence of the FDIC precedence over even the interests of depositors whenever the two came into conflict.

Senior officials of the FDIC – and probably the large majority of its other employees as well – were always aware that there would be no second chance for deposit insurance at the national level if the kind of bank losses that had characterized the years 1930-33 suddenly washed away the FDIC. After all, the eight state-formed deposit guarantee systems established between 1907 and 1917 had ceased operation with the onset of the Great Depression, or even earlier in some cases. Opponents of the new federal plan predicted a similar fate for the FDIC, with many reputable and competent persons and organizations taking this position. For example, the American Bankers Association called the FDIC legislation "unsound, unscientific, unjust and dangerous." There were many others even less complementary. It is not surprising that so many in the FDIC were determined to see to it that nationwide deposit insurance would survive.

An illustration of the strength of the "third mission" is found in a now forgotten piece of FDIC policy: the decision to interpret its statute as strictly as possible so as to hold payments to depositors in failed banks to a minimum. This was not a popular program, even within the FDIC. I recall being told by a former claim agent in the FDIC that he had sought and received a transfer because he could no longer bear to look into the eyes of a depositor who had just been told that he would receive much less than he had been expecting.

The policy adopted was simple and quite within the law. The FDIC was required to determine the amount of an insured balance by deducting any debt to the bank itself (which, of course, would now be a debt to the receiver, generally the FDIC). However, appropriate liquidation procedures and policy did not permit the FDIC to deduct a debt that was current, such as the remaining payments to be made on an installment loan to purchase an automobile, for which payments had been made regularly until the day the bank failed. However, another provision of the law allowed the FDIC to withhold any amount due the depositor if there existed a remaining debt of any kind. Depositors were, therefore, told that if they wanted immediate payment of their "insured" deposit, they could sign a "voluntary" request to reduce their deposit by the amount of the remaining payments.

Depositors in failed banks viewed the policy as outrageous. I recall one occasion when a Congressman or Congresswoman from a western state came storming into the FDIC because a bank that had failed in his or her district was in a remote area. Almost everyone had loan balances with the bank, many of them current and not subject to be offset. Yet insurance payments were being withheld, thus causing a very large number of angry depositors, and one very angry member of Congress.

Of course, there was no great saving to the FDIC from the policy because, ironically, there were so few bank failures, attributable in part to the times and in part to the diligence of the FDIC in its examination procedures. I mention this only because it was indicative of the importance attached by the FDIC to conserving all possible cash in anticipation of heavy payments yet to come. Incidentally, for those who may wonder if the FDIC still does this, its 50-year history, which I have mentioned before, said: "Eventually, vocal protests from irate depositors and prodding by some consumer activists persuaded the FDIC to abandon the policy in 1964."

The problems faced by the FDIC after World War II ended were not any easier. Indeed, they must have seemed immense. Not only was there the expectation by virtually everyone that there would be a horrendous post-war depression that would involve some large banks and quite possibly kill the FDIC. But even if the opposite happened, continued bank failures could be a critical problem in a period of general prosperity. After all, in the last prosperous period prior to World War II (1921-1929), bank failures in the United States averaged 600 per year and in one year (1928) actually came close to 1,000. There was no doubt that a high level of bank failures, even if most were small banks as had been the case in the 1921-29 period, could have a serious corrosive effect on confidence in the banking system. This meant that the system would likely be subject to severe pressures should an additional problem arise, as happened in the case of the collapse of the stock market in 1929 and the beginning of the long economic downturn. Accordingly, the attention of the FDIC turned toward the possibility of protecting federal deposit insurance by seeing to it that a truly effective "lender of last resort" would be created.

Reconstruction Finance Corporation. As the nation's central bank, the Federal Reserve was generally understood to have the primary (and probably sole) responsibility for serving as the institution that would take decisive action in the event of a banking crisis – the lender of last resort. Particularly important in such instances was the possibility that sound banks could break under the pressure, which in turn would add even more fuel to the crisis. The trouble was that several of the 12 Federal Reserve Banks acted as if they were nothing more than ordinary commercial banks, caught in an economic downturn, and had no responsibility for anyone else other than themselves. In short, they simply wanted to batten down the hatches until the storm passed. Many commercial banks attempted to do this, of course, but this was not something that the Federal Reserve had been expected to do.

President Hoover sought to create a new lender of last resort by establishing the Reconstruction Finance Corporation, as I described earlier. Although the RFC did some effective work in making investments in bank capital, after the Bank Holiday had ended it was no longer in a position to play any real part as a true lender of last resort. As a matter of fact, the RFC itself was closed in 1957.

Interestingly, the FDIC had been likened specifically to a lender of last resort by Professor John Kenneth Galbraith. In 1975 he wrote that: "the FDIC was what the Federal Reserve had not succeeded in being – an utterly reliable lender of last resort." However, what Galbraith had in mind was the power given to the FDIC in 1935 to make loans to weak banks for the purpose of facilitating their acquisition by sound banks. The FDIC had used this power on several occasions prior to 1950, but a merger was required to use this tactic. The FDIC now wanted authority to make loans during a severe banking crisis with or without a resulting merger.

In the late 1940s, Congress began to put together a complete updating and revision of the original deposit insurance law. The FDIC suggested adding a new provision making it also a "lender of last resort" on the assumption that the Federal Reserve would be no more interested in fulfilling that responsibility in the 1950s than it had been in the 1930s. The provision suggested by the FDIC – Section 13(c) – was short and simple: "In order to prevent the closing of an insured bank or in order to reopen a closed insured bank, the Corporation, in the discretion of its Board of Directors, is authorized to make loans to, or purchase the assets of, such insured bank upon such terms or conditions as the Board of Directors may prescribe." In other words, the FDIC's Board would not have to consult with any other agency, such as the Federal Reserve, nor did it need to obtain full security for any of its loans as was the case when the Federal Reserve took action. Significantly, both the House and Senate agreed with the FDIC that such an addition must be made to the FDIC's authority, and also agreed with the language that the Corporation suggested.

Perhaps solely as a matter of preserving its prestige, the Fed fought against accepting the FDIC's language, suggesting a number of limiting words, such as requiring that the bank must be in "imminent" danger of failing. The Fed was unsuccessful in such efforts until the very end. Then someone – and it could only have been the Fed – succeeded in getting an addition to the wording by the Senate, which the House grudgingly accepted. This simply added a condition that the FDIC's Board of Directors had to meet – namely, that the Board must find that the "continued operation of such bank is essential to provide adequate banking service in the community."

The Fed vs. the FDIC. This was the killer. The Fed immediately let it be known that the change meant that the FDIC could deal with situations involving the only bank in a community, and that meant that it could only deal with a very small bank. For some strange reason, the FDIC Board and its attorneys concurred in this interpretation. Even so, rumor had it that the FDIC had promised the Fed not to use the new provision except in quite unusual situations. The FDIC kept that promise for 20 years. I can only guess that in 1950, those running the FDIC never understood the concern of a future banking crisis like the one in 1933 that could have only two possible results, either of which could be quite damaging to the FDIC. The first was that the Fed would simply continue in the posture that it had adopted in 1930-33 with respect to involvement in banking crises. The Fed seemed to think at that time that the need to quell a serious banking panic was not part of a central bank's responsibility, although everyone else seemed to feel quite differently. The alternative was that the Fed would henceforth insist on assuming the position of lender of last resort and, as the crisis manager, would make certain that the losses taken would be absorbed by the FDIC and not by the Federal Reserve. The FDIC preferred not to take a chance on either of those prospects.

Of course, it is quite possible that those in charge of the FDIC, after the Federal Deposit Insurance Act of 1950 had been signed into law, never really understood the reason for the provision. Shortly after leaving the FDIC, I received a telephone call from FDIC Chairman Erle Cocke, Sr., noting that I had either spoken publicly about, or written in one of my reports, that there was no need to take a narrow view of the power granted to the FDIC by Section 13(c) of its Act. His ability to act as the lender of last resort was still valid, and I counseled simply ignoring the current interpretation by his staff. The Chairman thanked me for that opinion and then called back in several days and said that in running this by his attorneys the view seemed to be that the current interpretation had been used or applied on a number of occasions since 1950 so that it had now become settled law. In short, the FDIC could only use its authority when dealing with a single bank in a specific community. However, the ending of the story is just a bit different.

In 1971, the Bank of the Commonwealth in Detroit, with assets in excess of $1 billion, found itself in deep trouble. It was the Federal Reserve – I was told privately – that now was urging the FDIC to use the provision that the Fed had succeeded in emasculating in 1950, thereby keeping the bank from being recorded as a failure. The Fed's interest was not hard to understand: the nation's first billion dollar bank failure was about to take place and the bank was a state-chartered member of the Federal Reserve System. For the Fed, then beginning a major effort to expand its regulation of banks at the expense of the Comptroller of the Currency, it would be terribly embarrassing to be connected to a major bank failure, particularly since the bank had, in fact, been poorly supervised. The Fed wanted no publicity about a failure of this kind hashed over by the press. It sought to cultivate the impression that being the central bank made it a superior bank regulator whereas, in fact, central banks which also acted as hands-on regulators – and very few did – were notoriously inept, as the Fed itself had demonstrated in the 1930s and subsequently. In any event, the FDIC's 1972 annual report mentions only a single bank failure, and it wasn't Bank of the Commonwealth. The listed failure was a small bank in Massachusetts. Also mentioned in the 1972 FDIC annual report was a $60 million, five-year loan to Michigan's Bank of the Commonwealth, designed to "rehabilitate the bank."

It is amusing now to read the decision by the FDIC, as recorded in its 1972 annual report. After stating that it decided to proceed under Section 13(c), which required the Board of Directors to find the bank essential in providing adequate banking service to the community, the FDIC Board then decided that in this case the Bank of the Commonwealth was essential to providing adequate banking service "to the black community in Detroit." In addition, it cited the bank's contribution to "commercial banking competition in Detroit and the upper Great Lakes Region." It said the FDIC also worried about "the effect [the bank's] closing might have had on public confidence in the nation's banking system." In other words, the FDIC did exactly what I had claimed it had the power to do all along. And in so doing, it made it clear that the FDIC was the appropriate crisis manager in such situations.

This became even more apparent in the years to follow as a number of large banks faced serious financial difficulties. Most of those cases, including the 1984 failure of Continental Illinois, the nation's eighth largest bank, also were handled through Section 13(c). However, in 1991 a new federal statute introduced a remarkably complex arrangement for handling giant bank failures, leaving it unclear whether the FDIC or the Federal Reserve would be in charge in the future.

Chapter Three
Ending the "Anarchy of Uncontrolled Banking"

Professor John Kenneth Galbraith of Harvard University wrote of federal deposit insurance legislation: "In all American monetary history, no legislative action brought such a change as this." After briefly describing the key features of the 1933 legislation, he concluded with: "The anarchy of uncontrolled banking had been brought to an end, not by the Federal Reserve System but by the obscure, unprestigious, unwanted Federal Deposit Insurance Corporation." Galbraith's language was, as always, elegant, but someone not steeped in banking history might miss the target he had in mind: the so-called "dual banking" system. The dual banking system was born in 1863-65 by the creation of the national banking system and the failure to shut down the state banking system. This left the United States with an arrangement under which the federal government and the individual states had separate and equal rights with respect to the chartering of banks and supervising the banks they had created.

When the Federal Reserve was established in 1913, all national banks were required to be members, but state banks had the option of remaining outside the System, supervised only by their state banking departments, or joining the System and being supervised by both the Federal Reserve and the state banking department. A relatively small number of state-chartered banks elected to join the Federal Reserve System, and those that did tended to be the larger banks. Those state banks that remained outside of the Federal Reserve System have usually constituted half or more of all operating U.S. commercial banks. But state non-member banks were generally of small size so that they typically account for only about 15 to 20 percent of total bank assets.

With the exception of a few states, supervision of state non-member banks usually was poorly funded, and its quality could only be regarded as fair, at best. As a result, an extraordinarily large number of such banks were virtually free of any effective state government supervision, and corruption was not unknown in the state regulatory system. Not surprisingly, therefore, state non-member banks constituted 80 percent of all failed banks in 1930-32, and their deposits amounted to 57 percent of all the deposits in failed banks. Moreover, both of these percentages would likely have been even higher if one adds the additional 4,000 banks that had closed in early 1933, or had failed to reopen after the March 1933 Bank Holiday.

In late 1932, shortly before the final crash in March 1933, few persons would have disagreed with the assessment of the U.S. banking system made by Eugene Meyer, Governor of the Federal Reserve Board (since 1935, titled Chairman of the Board of Governors) and Sen. Carter Glass (D-Va.), often described as the "father" of the Federal Reserve. They were discussing the gloomy banking situation during a Senate hearing, and the exchange between them was:

> Glass: I think the curse of the banking system in this country is the dual system.

> Meyer: . . . and the Board is entirely in sympathy with the [Senate Banking] Committee on this.

Chairman Meyer later recommended to the Senate Banking Committee that only national banks should be allowed in the future and obtained an opinion from the Board's General Counsel that such legislation would be constitutional. However, no action was ever taken.

Neither Meyer nor Glass got his way. State-chartered banking was preserved, but the old state-federal system largely disappeared with the establishment of the FDIC. To be sure, the states retained their own banking codes so there were certain advantages attached to a state charter that attracted many banks, just as there were advantages to national charters. However, on the essentials, there was really nothing of significance left of the state banking system. It was the FDIC that, in effect, decided whether applicants for a state charter could enter the banking business, unless they intended to operate without federal deposit insurance, which was unlikely. Moreover, it was the FDIC that examined and regulated state non-member banks, although it was thought politically wise to act as though the states were still the principal supervisors. The circle was finally closed in 1991, during still another banking crisis, when the Federal Deposit Insurance Corporation Improvement Act (FDICIA) provided that any new powers given to state-chartered banks had to be approved by the FDIC if they exceeded powers not available to national banks.

It is important, however, to recognize that the old dual system was continued with respect to the kinds of options that were available to banks. The difference was that options were provided only by the federal government, using several agencies to do so. For example, the option as to whether to operate under a state banking code or a national banking code was still available as was the option to switch when one code appeared to be more useful than the other. Similarly, by changing charters bankers had the option of changing their regulator, so that, for example, a state-chartered non-member bank, if unhappy with the FDIC, could find a new supervisor by changing to a national charter, or by keeping its state charter but joining the Federal Reserve System. Similarly, a national bank could switch to Federal Reserve supervision as a state-chartered member bank, or to the FDIC as a state-chartered non-member bank. In that sense, therefore, the dual banking system continues, with a valuable degree of flexibility that would otherwise be impossible. But it continues at the sufferance of the federal government. It is surprising that more than a few state officials still act as though there are two separate and equal systems – state and national – or at least they pretend to believe it, but this is not the case and is only a source of continuous irritation and needless litigation.

There was, I should mention, a strong movement in 1965 by the State Bank Division of the American Bankers Association, supported by the National Bank Division, to rally state support for upgrading state banking in all of its aspects – funding and powers particularly. ABA's President, Archie K. Davis, Chairman of the Wachovia Bank and Trust Company, then one of the nation's leading state banks, led the campaign. As the Secretary of the State Bank Division then, I can testify to the immense effort that was made to help create a state banking system of the highest quality – free of federal government subsidy and of the regulation that came with it. However, the federal subsidy, (i.e., no charges for FDIC or Federal Reserve examinations and supervision) turned out to be too tempting for most states.

When World War II ended in 1945, the FDIC's Division of Examination was still in the process of building its examination force to an appropriate level. In the earliest days, it must have been an unbelievably difficult job. For example, in 1935, the second year in which the FDIC was in operation, it had only 534 employees in its examination division (both examiners and support staff), almost all of whom were distributed among regional offices. Yet in that year the Corporation completed one regular examination for each of 7,110 banks not members of the Federal Reserve System, in addition to 258 repeat examinations of many of the same banks, and 231 examinations of new banks applying for admission to deposit insurance. The annual report does mention that the FDIC examiners cooperated with certain of the states in lightening the examination load on the banks, so it must be assumed that the FDIC received some assistance from some of the state agencies. But presumably the FDIC's new Division of Examination did most of the work that I just described.

The seven years between the opening of the FDIC for business and the entry of the United States into World War II were not quiet years. In those seven years there were 375 bank failures, not all of which were very small banks. In 1935, the FDIC had only 25 persons in what was then called the "New and Closed Bank Division." This is the unit that, I presume, later became the Division of Liquidation. The Legal Division had a total of 17 persons in that early year, which included all staff, (both secretaries and attorneys). In short, it must have been an extremely difficult task for the FDIC to accomplish much of anything in its first years, but it did and I assume that the Division of Examination, with its 534 employees, constituting almost 75 percent of all employees in the FDIC, was what made it all work.

For the most part, the failures during these early years were of weak banks that had, nonetheless, been able to survive for a bit longer after the 1933 storm had passed. However, the Corporation was faced with other problems. For example, in 1937-38, while still mired in the 1930-33 depression, the country was hit by the shortest but deepest recession in our history. This occurred when the Federal Reserve, always worrying about inflation (which seemed preposterous given the condition of the country and the banks in 1937-38), abruptly doubled reserve requirements for all member banks, thereby touching off this second major decline.

As I noted earlier, World War II put an end to banking problems for a time. It was not until 1946 that the FDIC's Division of Examination faced once again the significant new responsibility of dealing with the "anarchy of uncontrolled banking." I rather suspect that the examining staff of the Corporation found this description quite accurate. The Corporation had a great pool of former bankers and regulators from which to draw in 1933 (including from the Reconstruction Finance Corporation), and those selected came to the new regulatory agency more or less as the harbingers of reform. They tended to view themselves as coming to "cleanse the stables" of poor bank supervision and regulation. Their nearly unanimous view was that all of the bank failures in the 1930s were solely the result of poor supervision.

That was not the case, of course. But there is no question that poor supervision had been a significant contributor. In any event, FDIC examiners were quite condescending toward the other federal regulators. The attitude of the Corporation's examiners seemed to be that the FDIC had little to learn from agencies such as the Office of the Comptroller of the Currency or the Federal Reserve, both of which, in their view, had done an exceedingly poor job during the Great Depression and now would have to be given a lesson about "real" examinations. Toward the states and their regulatory offices, the FDIC's attitude was a mixture of amusement bordering on contempt, although there were a few important exceptions, such as New York State. Officially, of course, the Corporation's public attitude toward the state agencies was always friendly and supportive. It was, after all, the existence of these agencies that bolstered the power of the FDIC in Washington.

Fortunately, the much-feared postwar depression never materialized. I think the realization that it would not appear at all probably occurred in late 1949 or 1950. I say this because when I arrived at the FDIC in early 1951, there was a gentleman in an office across the hall from me who seemed to have nothing to do, but was quite friendly and clearly would have delighted in having been given something to do. When I inquired, I found that he was the last of a number of potential senior officers at the FDIC who had been "stockpiled" in anticipation of the great postwar depression. The gentleman to whom I have referred had been persuaded to come over from the Reconstruction Finance Corporation. It was not very long after I arrived that he left to become an advisor on banking or financial matters to a middle-eastern country.

The record compiled by the Division of Examination during the next 25 years – say, from 1945 through 1969 – was astounding. The total number of banks failing in those years was 89, a little more than three per year. The most frequent explanation of this was that times had been very good, prosperity was here, and one would, of course, expect very few bank failures. Yet, as I described earlier, in a similar period, the one following the conclusion of a major war in 1918, there had been another prosperous period, sometimes described as the "Roaring Twenties." Unemployment was very low, the country was booming and the stock market appeared determined to make wealthy people out of millions of humble investors. Yet there were 5,711 bank failures, or more than 600 in each year on average, during that decade. In my view, the difference between 1921-29 and 1945-69 was the presence of the FDIC in the later period – particularly the FDIC's Division of Examination. If prizes could have been awarded for outstanding supervision and regulation, the FDIC would have found itself surfeited with silver loving cups, or whatever medals were used.

How did this happen in that crucial "quiet period" of 1945 through 1969? Because of my responsibility for editing the FDIC's annual report, I was in frequent contact with the Examination Division. The Division members with whom I spent the most time tended to be senior review examiners, stationed in Washington, almost all of whom had been with the FDIC from its first days. Just listening to their stories was an education in itself. An incident of minor importance provided an opportunity for me to request a temporary transfer to the Examination Division, the purpose being to improve my understanding of the role of that office in the course of preparing the FDIC's annual report. I reported to the Division of Examination in 1955, and was sent to the FDIC's District Five, headquartered in Atlanta. From there I was sent to the Jackson, Miss., sub-office, which took care of Mississippi, Western Alabama and occasionally the most northern part of Florida. That sub-office was headed by one of the top examiners in the FDIC, recognized as such by everyone, and I suspect he was the reason I was sent there.

The relationship between FDIC examiners in the field and the bankers they supervised was fascinating. In many instances the FDIC acted as if it were a consulting organization, albeit one with considerable clout. Examiners walked with a very heavy tread at that time in District Five, and they were not always gracious or friendly or understanding. This was particularly the case when a bank's problems were found to be attributable to financial irregularities by bank officers. Keeping in mind that most of the banks examined by the FDIC were quite small, particularly in Mississippi and Alabama, examiners tended to regard bankers who did a good job more or less as their equals, sharing the same basic objective – namely, the operation of a sound, reasonably profitable bank. Remember that about 70 percent of all commercial banks in the United States in the early 1950s had total deposits of less than $5 million. Banks in the largest deposit size group – those having deposits between $2 million and $5 million – paid officers on average a little less than $5,000 per year. Other employees earned about $2,000. I don't recall examiner salaries (I had kept my Research Division salary) except that while examiner salaries, like all salaries at the FDIC at that time, were pretty low, in most instances they probably were significantly higher than the amount paid to bank officers or employees in Mississippi and Alabama banks.

When bankers were not up to snuff in the eyes of the FDIC examiners, they found ways to instruct and advise, sometimes nicely and sometimes not so nicely. For example, one time we visited and examined two banks in the same week in a reasonably prosperous section of Mississippi. In the first bank, the examiner-in-charge seemed to go out of his way to find loans that he could list under "special mention" (potentially troublesome) and other loans that he classified as "substandard." This was not true in the second bank, but I could not see a particle of difference between the two banks, or in the areas they served, or in the nature of their loans. When we returned to the district sub-office in Jackson, I asked him how his decisions had been made. His answer was that the first bank was family-owned (very often the case, of course) and that the old President had been an outstanding banker, but had died quite unexpectedly. The new President was his son, a teacher at a local high school. The examiner thought it essential to shape up the son by requiring him to investigate closely a great many loans and, moreover, respond to the inevitable questions that would be posed once the examination report was given to the Board of Directors. The Board, seeing all those loan classifications was likely to be on the new President's back from the moment the examiners left the bank – especially because, as I recall, Mississippi law at the time exposed directors to some residual liability on loans they had approved. The FDIC examiner told me that we had left with a very unhappy Board of Directors, but that he expected that when he returned next year he would find a much wiser President at the annual bank examination. I checked later and, in fact, found that this had happened.

It was then that I began to understand fully why, back in Washington, it had been decided that we should drop from the FDIC's annual report some figures that we published regularly since 1934, showing examiner evaluations of loans, grouped by states and size of bank. The argument that I heard in Washington was that for some kinds of banks, particularly small banks and in some parts of the country, the figures on classified assets were meaningless. The basic criticism was that individual examiners would differ in their approach to classifications. But also, examiners might use loan classifications for a variety of purposes, having nothing to do with the real quality of the loan, as happened in this case.

In the 1950s, virtually all bank failures resulted from defalcations or losses attributable to financial irregularities by officers or employees. This had not been the case in the early 1930s, when the principal causes of bank failures were mismanagement, deteriorating local economic conditions and an inability to restore a bank's financial position that had been seriously impaired by the 1930-33 crisis. The situation was much different in the 1950s, so much so that when a bank in Maine failed in 1955 because of a deteriorating asset situation resulting from "adverse local economic conditions," there had been an excited buzz in the corridors in Washington. People were talking of a "real" failure having just occurred – namely, one that could not be attributed to defalcation or mismanagement, but simply to a sudden and unexpected collapse in, as I recall, potato prices.

FDIC examiners focused intently on discovering and removing bank officers or other employees guilty of financial irregularities or, in some cases, simply guilty of sheer inability to manage a bank. However, since a bank examination is not an audit, the principal job of the examiner was to value the assets of the bank, to compute the net sound capital after making the necessary asset adjustments required by the examination, and to take whatever action was needed when the recomputed capital was found to be inadequate. Fraud was not something that an examiner was expected to discover or deal with, in theory at least. Thus, the FDIC examiners made a serious and coordinated effort to detect suspicious actions that might lead to defalcations. I think it was about that time that I developed, personally, a conviction that has stayed with me through all the years since. Bank capital is not the most important factor in any examination, I concluded. The most important factor by far is the quality of management.

Although I was only in the field for perhaps four or five months, I do recall three or four incidents when the sole objective was to remove an individual from the bank because of a suspicion on the part of examiners that the person was engaged in irregular or fraudulent activities or, in one case, was simply so inept that he shouldn't be in banking. In one instance, the fact that I was new and did not speak "Southern" was used to advantage by the examiner-in-charge. My recollection is that this was the reexamination then required when an "involuntary termination of insurance action" had been brought against the bank earlier. Once again, loan classifications were to help make it possible to achieve the intended result. The examiners in prior examinations suspected that the Chief Executive Officer was involved in a serious kite and wanted the Board to remove him. A kite is the practice of depositing and drawing checks at two or more banks and taking advantage of the lapse of time before the second bank collects funds from the first bank.

My assignment in this instance was to go to the office of the President of the bank and to ask to be provided with the most recent seven or eight prior examination reports, along with a place in which I could review them. My instruction from the examiner in charge was simply to begin reading very carefully, making notes if I found anything interesting, but showing the notes to no one and, mostly, to refuse to answer any question about whom I was or what I was doing. This was not difficult at first since I did not have the faintest idea why I was doing what I was doing, and had trouble understanding the intricacies of an examination report. I also was instructed to answer any question as to where I came from or what I was there for by saying: "I am from the Washington office." This was, of course, quite correct. The examiners had a different purpose in mind, which was to so upset the banker that he would not be able to defend himself successfully to the Board of Directors. By the morning of the second day, he was continually dropping into the room I had been provided to chat or ask what I was looking for. When he did not receive an answer, sweat beads of worry began to appear on his forehead, particularly when I stressed my Washington connection. I was told later when we left the bank that the examiner-in-charge, after classifying as many, if not more, assets then he had earlier, had met with the Board of Directors and urged that they find a new President. Since the examination had revealed that a kite of some consequence was probably being run, the Directors immediately complied.

Of all of the other incidents, the one that sticks most vividly with me was a meeting of the FDIC examiners in the Fifth District head office in Atlanta. There was excited talk about a recent case in which one of the examiners suspected that collateral for a loan to a large borrower, a friend of the bank President, was fictitious. One night the examiner somehow gained entry to the warehouse in which the collateral was stored, took a flash photograph which showed that the warehouse was empty and brought a photo back to the bank. When the President saw the photo, he immediately resigned. I was curious as to how this examiner had been able to get into the warehouse late at night and take pictures, but I did not inquire too closely. There was no question that he was treated as a hero at that particular meeting.

Actually, one could not be at the FDIC very long in the 1950s without hearing stories about a remarkably able crew of examiners, I think headquartered in St. Louis. This group worked only on particularly difficult cases involving bank officers that the FDIC felt the bank would be better without. The crew was a sort of roving "swat" team, and the examiner who headed it was called in whenever there seemed no other way of dealing with a particularly tough situation. The chief examiner of the team had a reputation for being threatening, frightening and even abusive to suspected errant bankers. My guess is that the stories about his tactics were embroidered and that his record of success probably was padded a bit. But not by very much; he was a legend at the FDIC. Very recently, after checking with a few other old-timers just to see if my memory was accurate, I was assured that, yes indeed, he did exist and, yes indeed, that establishing a kind of FDIC swat team to deal with the principal reason for bank failures in the 1950s and 1960s – defalcations and financial irregularities by bank officers – had been a necessary and effective move. I did not ask if something similar still existed, but I would not be shocked to find, even today, that it does.

Summarizing, the FDIC in the 1950s was a small, tightly managed federal agency, focused on its assigned mission to restore to depositors in failed banks the amount of their insured deposits. It had been created at the end of possibly the worst banking crisis in U.S. history. The philosophy of the FDIC examiners at the time was simplicity itself: the best way to protect depositors against loss due to bank failures (and, just incidentally, to protect the FDIC itself) was to stop all bank failures. Due in substantial part to its own efforts, the Division of Examination succeeded in raising the standards of bank supervision and regulation throughout the nation, most particularly in a poorly regulated portion of the banking industry in the United States.

Or, to use Professor Galbraith's words, it ended the "anarchy of uncontrolled banking."

In my opinion, the examining staff at the FDIC did a remarkable job in closing a gaping hole in the regulatory system produced by the existence of the dual banking system. However, I must concede that some of the things that I observed, several of which I have described, would not be possible today. There is no question that the FDIC in that period was an extremely strict regulatory agency and, conceivably, even stricter than was required.

I am reminded of a famous incident on this point. In 1962, the FDIC finally acquired its own building, a rather handsome edifice at the corner of New York Avenue and 17th Street NW in Washington, quite close to the old Executive Office Building, which sits just west of the White House. The opening of the FDIC's new building was celebrated in an elaborate ceremony, with the invited guests seated during a particularly nice day on the large plaza in front of the building, and the speakers seated at a dais. The principal speaker was the Chairman of the House Banking and Currency Committee, Rep. Wright Patman (D-Tex.). I was one of the invited guests in the audience even though I had left the FDIC several years before.

Patman was a long-time Chairman of the Banking Committee and a certified populist. He knew a great deal about banking and did not share the ABA's reverence for Federal Reserve independence. Indeed, he was continually trying to limit or end the Fed's independence. Large banks were another favorite target of his, and he did not hold the American Bankers Association in high regard. His talk was quite remarkable.

One of the boasts of the FDIC for at least the 10 to 15 years prior to 1962 was the fact that there had been remarkably few bank failures, and that all of these had been of small size. To be sure, the post-war economy may have been largely accountable for this, but certainly the FDIC's notably tough examining staff, which cracked down early and quickly at any sign of a banking problem, made an important contribution. Word of that toughness had spread with remarkable speed among bankers. It was this record to which Patman directed his attention, and not at all favorably. Essentially, the Texas Congressman suggested, in a manner that only he could do, that the FDIC was too interested in preserving and protecting its deposit insurance fund and not interested enough in seeing to it that the borrowers – such as small farmer constituents in his east-Texas district – were able to obtain loans. He then made what to others sitting on the dais was a truly astonishing statement – namely, that the FDIC should look for ways to loosen up and permit occasional bank failures, in order to assure us that bankers were taking the kinds of risks that were expected of them.

The faces of the top FDIC officials were remarkable to observe. Apoplectic is possibly the closest word I can find. I do know that there were smiles on several faces in the audience, including mine. Patman's idea was not foreign to bank economists, but quite clearly it had never occurred to anyone sitting on the dais with the speaker that day.

Chapter Four
Clark Warburton: Pioneer Monetarist

One of the few benefits of the Great Depression of the 1930s and the banking disaster that occurred in its midst was that they remarkably focused the attention of those who were expected to pick up the pieces. There were many such persons and institutions in Washington then and among the most prominent were Clark Warburton and the new Federal Deposit Insurance Corporation.

In several preceding chapters, I have described how the FDIC reacted when it discovered that the United States possessed no "lender-of-last-resort," willing to lend freely, even at high rates if necessary, to sound banks threatened by a looming financial catastrophe. To be sure, it had been assumed that our central bank (the Federal Reserve) had this responsibility, but, as things turned out, the Fed was unwilling to act, even when asked to do so by President Hoover. Thus, late in his Administration Mr. Hoover was compelled to ask Congress to charter a new "lender-of-last-resort," the Reconstruction Finance Corporation. Congress did so, but too late for it to be very useful before the crash came in March 1933.

Another problem highlighted by the banking collapse was the fact that large numbers of state-chartered banks had been receiving virtually no supervision, so that even during the palmy years of 1921-29 the number of bank failures averaged about 600 per year. Then in the next four years more than 9,000 banks failed, the large majority of which (probably at least 80 percent) were state-chartered non-member banks. Consequently, when the FDIC opened for business in 1934, the FDIC's examiners moved to close this gaping hole, with the single-minded determination that the only way to assure that the FDIC would have sufficient resources to handle its deposit insurance commitment was to make certain that the number of bank failures was reduced to as close to zero as possible.

One of the offices in the FDIC that had an important role to play was the Division of Research and Statistics. Like the Corporation as a whole, it was motivated by the objective to discover what had gone wrong in the early 1930s and, to the extent possible, to make sure that it would not happen again. In this regard, the Division of Research and Statistics asked one of its senior economists, Dr. Clark Warburton, to identify the research areas most in need of attention. He responded by suggesting, and outlining, a multi-faceted long-term study project: "The Causes of Bank Failures and the Relation of Banking to Business Fluctuations." Along with many others, Warburton had been shocked at the government's seeming helplessness in the face of an oncoming banking crisis. In a later year he wrote that his recommendation of such a study was made because "the continued future solvency of the Corporation appeared to be contingent on the absence of severe depressions."

The Warburton proposal was adopted by the FDIC in 1935 and announced publicly in 1936. The proposed study dealt with fundamental policy questions which, for their resolution, went far beyond the abilities or responsibilities of just the FDIC. As things turned out, it was to have a greater impact than anyone could have anticipated.

A Brilliant Mind. I met Clark Warburton for the first time in 1951, on the day that I arrived at the FDIC. I was alone in the city since my wife was handling our move from Rockland County, N.Y., and as soon as he found this out Clark invited me to have dinner with him and his wife that evening. This was the beginning of a long, friendly relationship. Actually, it was more than that; to put no finer point on it, during my half century in banking I had the good fortune to meet and work with a few truly outstanding individuals of whom Clark Warburton was most assuredly one. However, my main interest was in economic history, primarily with the resolution of public policy issues by bankers and government regulators, and not in monetary policy. For Clark's work in monetary economics, most of which had been done before I came to the FDIC, I had the utmost admiration, although "awe" might be the better word. In any event, Clark liked to obtain comments on drafts of his latest articles and of major pieces of correspondence. I was delighted to help because for me it meant, over the years, a priceless education in monetary economics. My comments almost always dealt with editorial matters such as emphasis, relevance and so forth. Many years later I have great difficulty remembering any occasion when I challenged Clark's position on an issue that he was addressing.

Apparently Clark came rather late in life to the subject of money and banking. He began his professional career as a lecturer in economics at the University of Allahabad, in India, in the early 1920s. Later he held several college or university positions in the United States as an instructor or professor of economics. He obtained his Ph.D., from the Faculty of Political Science at Columbia University. His thesis was titled *The Economic Results of Prohibition* and was published by the Columbia University Press in 1932. He was a member of the research staff of the Brookings Institution, a noted Washington think-tank, in 1932-33 and came to the FDIC in 1934. There was nothing I could see that indicated any special interest in banking or finance.

In a conversation about his thesis subject, I once asked Clark how he happened to develop an interest in banking. He chuckled and said that his book on the economics of Prohibition might have become a great seller among those engaged in the production or sale of illegal alcohol, except that Prohibition ended in 1933. Then addressing my question more seriously, he said that during the Great Depression his wife had obtained a teaching position in a local public school and had asked each member of one of her classes (my guess is fourth or fifth graders) to write a short essay on the single most important event in their lives. Clark was helping her grade the essays and said that he was deeply impressed by the fact that so many of the students had selected the failure of their local banks as the most important event in their lives.

The first task assigned to Clark when he arrived at the FDIC was to work with a group asked to recommend an assessment rate to be paid by banks holding insured deposits. That effectively meant all banks. In 1934 and part of 1935, the FDIC was operating under a temporary deposit insurance plan, and its funds had been provided by investments in its capital stock by the Federal Reserve and the U.S. Treasury, plus an assessment on insurable deposits of one-half of one percent. The study conducted by Clark's group had all the earmarks of a Warburton project – a close, detailed examination of bank failures and depositor losses during the 70 years from 1863 (when the national banking system was organized under the National Bank Act) until 1933. A significant amount of data was available, much of which had never been thoroughly examined, particularly with a focus on the size of banks and losses to depositors. That study was completed and presented to the Board of Directors of the FDIC, which accepted its recommendations and presented them to the House and Senate Banking Committees in Congress. There, the recommendations were adopted with little change and incorporated in the Banking Act of 1935.

The study had concluded that an assessment rate on total domestic deposits of one-twelfth of one percent on all participating banks would have been sufficient over the 70-year period except for three major depressions, those of the 1870s, the 1890s and, of course, the 1930s. Although the study did not go further back than 1863, bank historians have generally recognized that the depression from 1839 to 1842, touched off by the Panic of 1837, was at least as severe as 1930-33 and was another depression for which the suggested formula would not have provided sufficient funds.

The report's reservations with respect to very serious depressions were made quite clear, and the full report was included in the first annual report of the FDIC. Actually, the Board of Directors of the FDIC had been concerned from the outset about the possibility of insufficient funds to cover bank failures, and early on urged that the FDIC be given the power to "examine its risk," as Leo T. Crowley, the second FDIC Chairman, liked to put it. Crowley had in mind, among other things, subjecting to FDIC examination and supervision the state-chartered banks that were not members of the Federal Reserve. Such banks accounted for well over half of all banks in the United States, although holding only about 20 percent of total bank deposits. The FDIC, in fact, obtained that authority from Congress.

It was clear that Clark Warburton was quite proud of the study and the assessment formula he and his group had devised. It provided a great deal of information and data never before collected nor rigorously analyzed for the purpose of understanding the cost of bank failures to depositors, to stockholders and, now, to the federal government. Indeed, except for an ill-advised change in 1950 providing assessment credits to banks during years with few bank failures, my guess is that the system would still be in place early in the 21st century. In any event, the old system did quite well for 54 years, more than a half century.

Earlier, I mentioned Clark Warburton's recommendation in 1935 that the FDIC's Division of Research and Statistics launch a multi-faceted study called "The Causes of Bank Failures and the Relation of Banking to Business Fluctuations." The final piece of that study was of particular interest to Clark, having to do with the effect of national monetary policy on bank failures. In the "Introduction" to a volume containing his selected papers, published by the Johns Hopkins University Press in 1966, Clark described how, by 1945, he had reached a position that would serve as the basis for virtually all of his future work on banking and business fluctuations.

As Clark put it, he embraced the theory of "monetary disequilibrium," which held that "substantial departures from a stable or steadily growing stock of money at a reasonable rate is the major element in bringing about depression or inflation . . ." In short, he was a monetarist. To be sure, Clark Warburton did not invent monetarism, referring to it as a "venerable theory," but one that had been ignored or forgotten once a large portion of the economics profession took up with enthusiasm the theories of John

Maynard Keynes. Nor was Clark the only economist with monetarist views or inclinations, although in the 1940s these were not numerous.

In fact, Clark began his own campaign at the very height of the profession's enthusiasm for the work of Keynes. Clark was insisting in his articles that "money does count," in the sense that change in the money supply is the dominant originating cause of inflation or depression, something that the Keynesians clearly did not believe. Clark also was insisting that monetary policy was a potent tool. If used wisely, it could produce successful results, but if used poorly – as he claimed was the fact in the early 1930s – it could lead to disaster. He produced approximately 25 articles between 1945 and 1953, usually heavily buttressed by data. Virtually all were published by the most prestigious professional journals in economics, such as the *Journal of Political Economy*, the *Quarterly Journal of Economics*, the *Journal of Finance*, and the *American Economic Review*.

In describing his articles, Clark made it clear that they were not successive reports on the progress of work in the program he had suggested for the FDIC's Division of Research and Statistics in 1935, although they did embrace some of the significant results of that work. Instead, he said that work had served as stimuli for his articles, each of which he wrote personally, carefully noting in each instance that the article was Clark's own view and was not to be construed as the view of the FDIC.

Clark's articles were strongly written, making it clear that he had little confidence in the work currently being done by the overwhelming majority of economists on the matter of banking and business fluctuations. One of his best-known articles was directed at the economics profession. In it he noted that "the most remarkable feature of contemporary business fluctuation theory is the unanimity with which economists have ignored the timing and amplitude of changes in the quantity of money in the United States relative to changes in population, output, consumer spending, prices and employment." He then attached the longest footnote I have ever encountered – two and one-half pages in small type, setting forth the full names of about 85 erring economists, including virtually all of the then best-known members of the profession, and referencing many of their recent articles.

In more than a few articles Clark was quite critical of the Federal Reserve. For example, he wrote that: "Extreme monetary maladjustments have occurred since the establishment of the Federal Reserve and those maladjustments are primarily responsible for the violence of economic fluctuations during the past three decades (referring most importantly to the depression of 1933, but also to those of 1921 and 1938). In other words, contrary to expectations in 1913, the Federal Reserve itself had turned out to be the primary source of economic instability. In another article (published in 1945) he demonstrated that with a correct monetary policy the downturn in 1929 would have ended most probably in the autumn of 1930. Moreover, he said then, "in an economic climate from which the paralyzing pressure of monetary contraction had been removed," business would have continued at a high level, perhaps with moderate fluctuations. In other words, he claimed the disaster of 1930-33 was primarily the responsibility of the Federal Reserve.

One would have expected Clark's articles to touch off furious debate. Not so. There was only silence. Apparently his timing was simply bad. The general reaction by the economics profession appeared to be that his articles were no longer relevant in the new environment and, therefore, need not be addressed.

By 1953, Clark was planning to review his articles to take into account additional information available for the post-World War II period. However, the FDIC's Board of Directors suddenly decided to suspend all work on his study. Later, Clark wrote that the suspension lasted until about 1962-63, at which time he had been detailed to the House Banking Committee, which requested a statement from him to be used in forthcoming hearings focusing on the Federal Reserve. At the same time, he noted that review of his earlier writings had thus far provided no reason to alter his basic conclusions.

Clark's account did not provide any reason for the suspension of his publications for almost 10 years. There were some who thought it possible that Clark may have decided to quit writing merely because of the cold reception given to his articles written from 1945 to 1953. I doubt that. I am certain that Clark continued his research; he just simply ceased to write-up and publish the results. Clark was a driven, dedicated man when it came to the importance of his work and was quite capable of putting in 14 to 18 hours a day when necessary. I have no doubt that the decision to rein Clark in was made by the FDIC Board of Directors, probably in response to pressure from the outside. My only recollection (and a quite hazy one after more than 50 years) was some talk in 1953 that a speech given in Washington by Clark had upset some people, but just who was upset I cannot recall. In any event, the decision on publication was quite upsetting to all of us who were his colleagues but, on the other hand, there was no question that by 1953 the bulk of his best work had already been written and published.

I suppose it is possible that if there had been no interruption in the flow of articles, the end of what I have termed the economics profession's "wall of silence" toward Clark would have come earlier. However, word had spread rapidly of what appeared to be a ban imposed by the FDIC on the preparation of further articles by Clark, and the news upset a good many people. I was frequently asked when attending various conferences who or what was behind this, but I could not respond because I simply did not know. But it did strike me then, and still seems likely to me, that if the intention was to reduce the interest in Clark's ideas, it had quite the opposite effect.

For the "wall" did disappear finally, and I suppose any number of dates could be found to mark the occasion. My choice would be the publication in 1963 of the now classic *A Monetary History of the United States, 1867-1960* by Milton Friedman and Anna Jacobson Schwartz. It was impossible after the appearance of the Friedman-Schwartz volume to avoid the fact that an extremely strong case could be made for the possibility that money, indeed, "does count" and that the appropriate monetary policy conducted at the correct time was likely to be much more effective than merely "pushing on a string." And for those who pay attention to Prefaces, it was no longer possible to ignore Clark Warburton.

The authors of *A Monetary History* had a great many persons and organizations to thank for assistance in the preparation of their major study and the fact that they put Clark first on that long list, together with an explanation of why they did so, was significant. I am one who does read Prefaces and have used what they said about Clark in my own reports. Some others have done the same. Still, I think it is worth repeating it here.

> We owe an especially heavy debt to Clark Warburton. His detailed and valuable comments on several drafts have importantly affected the final version. In addition, time and again, when we came to some conclusion that seemed to us novel and original, <u>we found that he had been there before us</u>. (underscoring added)

Those final nine words – "we found that he had been there before us" – must have been welcome, but at the same time bittersweet praise for Clark. In his "A Tribute to Clark Warburton," a journal article written after Clark's death in 1979, Professor Thomas F. Cargill of the University of Nevada simply said: "He may not have coined the word monetarism, but he was the first monetarist of the post-World War II period."

I think it remarkable that many of the most important articles written by Clark, setting forth views that at the time were thought to be of dubious merit or not even worth considering, are now regarded as a solid, important part of the literature, usually introduced by something like: "It is now generally recognized that . . ." The responsibility of the Federal Reserve for the 1930-33 depression and the associated banking disaster is an excellent example.

One of Clark's articles that impressed me had appeared in *Econometrica* in April 1945 and was subsequently reprinted in several other journals. The title of his article was "Monetary Theory, Full Production and the Great Depression" and the relevant portion of the article was "The 1930s – What Might Have Been." In that section, Clark laid out in several pages the likely results of the 1930-33 turndown if it had been handled correctly by the Federal Reserve, which is to say it would have been a short depression probably ending, he said, in late 1930 or possibly in 1931. In short, the great disaster to banking and, more importantly, to the nation, would never have taken place. Almost 20 years later, in the Freidman-Schwartz *A Monetary History*, the authors devoted more than 100 pages to what they called "the Great Contraction." They called attention to Clark's 1945 article, as well as to three others written and published about the same time. Friedman-Schwartz brought to the subject an impressive amount of additional information and evidence. They arrived essentially at the same place that Clark had, stating: "the failure of the Federal Reserve System to prevent the collapse reflected not the impotence of monetary policy but rather the particular policies by the monetary authorities . . . The contraction is in fact a tragic testimony to the importance of monetary forces." My recollection, possibly incorrect, is that their conclusion was something of a shock to a good part of the economics profession when it first appeared. And although I also may be incorrect on this point, I don't recall ever seeing any formal attempt by the Federal Reserve to reexamine why it had acted the way it did during the decade of the 1930s.

Then another 40 years went by, during which there was a growing acceptance of the fact that the whole thing had been the Fed's fault. There was no doubt about this so far as Professor Allan Meltzer was concerned in Volume I of his widely-praised recent book, *A History of the Federal Reserve*. In a section titled: "Achievements and Failures," the discussion of failures begins with the statement that: "If the Federal Reserve had maintained monetary growth, the country and the world would have avoided years of depression." Meltzer went on: "Failure to act during the Great Depression was the Federal Reserve's largest error, but far from the only one." As for banking, he stated: "Nothing in theory or central banking practice can explain why the Federal Reserve did not respond to the failure of thousands of banks." Because Alan Greenspan, a former Chairman of the Federal Reserve Board, wrote a congratulatory "Forward" for Volume I, I think it may be assumed that the case is now closed. Except for a minor quibble and a personal note.

As for my quibble, if Clark Warburton were still alive I think it likely that he would have dropped a note to Professor Meltzer. The note may have pointed out that references to Clark's articles, which were not identified by title but simply by "Warburton 1966," refer to the 1966 volume containing all of Clark's *Selected Papers*. Thus, the reader would have no easy way of knowing that the particular papers referred to (the same as those identified by dates and titles in the Friedman-Schwartz *A Monetary History*) were written and published 20 years earlier, in 1944-46, when Clark stood virtually alone to level at the Federal Reserve this serious charge of culpability for the 1930-33 disaster.

As for the personal note, just glancing over the last several paragraphs, it strikes me that I and others may have been unduly harsh with the Federal Reserve. Let me be clear that I am not talking about today's Fed, which is quite different. Congress, for example, took care of a number of serious structural problems in the Banking Act of 1935. Moreover, even at the time the Fed's policies were consistent with the views of many, if not most, in the financial community, as well as with those of a majority of economists. The basic problem was that by the late 1920s the Federal Reserve possessed neither the administrative structure nor the quality of leadership required to deal with what was becoming increasingly obvious: the ensuing depression was likely to be the mother of all financial disasters. There were more than a few in the Federal Reserve itself who saw this clearly, as did others, such as the Secretary of the Treasury. For that matter, both President Roosevelt and President Hoover (but particularly President Hoover) sensed that something had gone terribly wrong. But the Federal Reserve, after the death in 1928 of Benjamin Strong, the outstanding Governor of the Federal Reserve Bank of New York, had lost its great *de facto* leader. The system then forgot that it was a central bank and not a collection of 12 regional commercial banks. So it circled its wagons and pulled over itself the sacred blanket of independence.

I did not see very much of Clark Warburton after I left the FDIC in 1960, particularly after he retired about five years later. That was my loss, with no real excuse except that I was deeply involved in creating Golembe Associates, Inc., a new bank consulting firm, during part of that time. Also, Clark went to California for a time to lecture at the University of California (Davis). He had resumed writing and submitting his articles for publication in the 1960s. Particularly important was the publication of the aforementioned *Selected Papers* in 1966. Each of the 19 chapters of that volume contained one of his finest pieces of work, all of them written and published between 1945 and 1953. The *Selected Papers* volume also contains an outstanding "Introduction," written by Clark himself. The Introduction described his intellectual journey to embracing the monetary disequilibrium theory, the work he thought still had to be done, and a prediction that if the rate of monetary expansion as of 1966 was continued, "a substantial future inflation is inevitable." That inflation arrived in 1979, the year Clark died.

Clark Warburton's death spawned an impressive number of memorials, several of which I have noted. The most useful for those who are unacquainted with Clark's influence and writings was the 65-page retrospective of Clark's contribution to monetary economics by Michael D. Bordo (Carleton University, Canada) and Anna J. Schwartz (National Bureau of Economic Research). Their concluding paragraph said:

> Warburton's early presentation of the case that "money matters" entitles him to the designation of Pioneer Monetarist . . . At the time that Warburton began to publish, events that would call into question the prevailing Keynesian orthodoxy had not yet unfolded. Those who were not persuaded years ago by Warburton's percipient analysis have lived to see events vindicate it.

Impressions and Recollections. My intention in the preceding section was to sketch lightly Clark Warburton's career without going into great detail on his writings, which were intended for economists and not for the general public (and, truth be told, not for all economic historians either). Whether I succeeded or not, résumés cannot give a full picture of an individual, and I thought it would be helpful if I ended this chapter with a small collection of personal stories involving Clark.

As word spread, slowly to be sure, of Clark Warburton's ideas, I was often asked what kind of person he was, or how he had managed to produce so many solidly researched articles in so short a time. After all, he had published at least 25 articles, appearing in the most prestigious professional journals, that challenged the view of the vast majority of economists when it came to the subject of banking and business fluctuations, or of the importance of monetary policy. Particularly impressive to many readers must have been the author's heavy reliance on data previously overlooked or never before presented in a new or surprising form, along with the clear evidence that he possessed a deep knowledge of the 19th and early 20th century material on the causes of business fluctuations, something that also had been forgotten or had been overlooked by other writers. All of this was presented in powerfully written form that seemingly left little room for debate.

Moreover, early in Clark's tenure the FDIC was a new agency, primarily concerned with picking up the pieces after bank failures occurred. It is not noted for having legions of economists, yet its Research Division was often critical of the Federal Reserve, which does have legions of economists, some quite well-known, as well as formal responsibility for the nation's monetary policy. Why should the FDIC concern itself?

I have explained why the FDIC, from the day it was created in 1933, was deeply interested in the conduct of monetary policy. Very simply, any repetition of the Fed's policy failures of the 1930-33 years would wipe out the Corporation. And even in its very early days, the Corporation was not lacking for good economists in addition to Clark. For example, Homer Jones, who briefly headed the FDIC's Research Division, was there before leaving to take a similar position at the Federal Reserve Bank of St. Louis, where he performed in an outstanding manner. But in the period of Clark's greatest productivity, 1945-53, he had no real help except secretarial and clerical assistance plus access to the FDIC statistical capabilities. With respect to the latter, I have the feeling that Clark was always deeply involved in assembling and interpreting the statistical material that served as the foundation for many of his articles. Often when dropping into his office I found him surrounded by stacks of statistical tables that he was either editing or examining closely, usually for implications that soon would appear in one of his articles.

In the article on Clark written by Professor Thomas F. Cargill, of the University of Nevada, he had addressed the question of why it took so long for Clark's work to win the appreciation it deserved. Cargill offered a variety of explanations, such as: "He was not part of an academic institutional framework, with graduate students that would further develop and market his ideas. He was a one-man show." I agree, and rather think that he preferred it that way. I don't believe Clark was worried about lacking the benefit of the collegiality of academia. Earlier I described his published criticism of about 90 academics who, he said, persisted in ignoring relevant data, something I think would have been difficult to do had he been teaching at a major university.

In his "Preface" to the volume of his *Selected Papers*, Clark presented only a single paragraph expressing his appreciation for assistance and, with only one exception, no individuals were identified, only government agencies. The agencies were thanked for the most part because they had provided Clark with unpublished data for him to use in preparing or developing his own statistical series. The lone individual I mentioned was in that group. Interestingly, Clark did not include the FDIC in the agencies to which he expressed appreciation, possibly for good reason, but he did reserve his warmest note of appreciation for the personnel of the FDIC's Division of Research and Statistics. I have often believed that it was because of the support and respect given Clark by most members of the Division – particularly by its Chief, Edison Cramer – that the effort to stifle Clark's publications did not go even further, perhaps even to dismissal.

This does not mean, however, that Clark was unaware of what was going on around him in his own world of monetary economics. My impression is that he had a large number of contacts, primarily outside of the FDIC since the Research Division was quite small. But Clark had been in Washington for 20 years when I got there and had ample opportunity, which I know that he used, to identify a collection of persons whose opinions he regarded highly.

Moreover, he was a great letter writer. For example, there was a period of several years during the 1950s when there was a heavy concentration of correspondence by letter between Clark and Milton Friedman. I became aware of this because Clark asked me to comment on several of his letters before they were mailed. All one has to do is peruse the Friedman-Schwartz *A Monetary History*, particularly the chapter titled "The Great Contraction, 1929-33," to find several references to Clark's thinking, some of which reflected, I am sure, the correspondence just mentioned.

Clark was always on the lookout for academicians he thought to be particularly able and sympathetic to his views. One of these was Professor Leland B. Yeager, who in 1962 edited *In Search of a Monetary Constitution*, published by the Harvard University Press. Clark was represented in this book by a substantial article: "Monetary Disturbances and Business Fluctuations in Two Centuries of American History." Yeager, a Ludwig Von Mises Distinguished Professor Emeritus at Auburn University, as well as Professor Emeritus of Economics at the University of Virginia, was asked by the Warburton family to write the Preface for Clark's final article, written shortly before Clark died.

The Bray Hammond Connection. It was through Clark that I met Bray Hammond, a long-time Assistant Secretary of the Federal Reserve Board. Bray had retired from that post in 1950 and was then spending a great deal of time putting together his superb history of American banking, *Banks and Politics in America: From The Revolution to The Civil War*. The centerpiece of his history, in my view at least, is the riveting account of the conflict between President Andrew Jackson and Nicholas Biddle, President of the Second Bank of the United States. Historians have long characterized the conflict as "The Bank War." It ended with the destruction of the Second Bank, our first real central bank, by President Jackson. Seventy-seven years were to pass before the United States again had a central bank with the establishment of the Federal Reserve System in 1913.

In the 1950s, Bray and I quickly became friends because of our mutual interest in economic history, as well as the fact that we both had been focused on banking history prior to the Civil War. The only difference – but a huge one – was that Bray was already a published historian of note whereas I had just completed my doctoral thesis in 1952 on pre-Civil War banking in five of our Midwestern states – Ohio, Indiana, Michigan, Illinois and Wisconsin.

Bray was interested in discussing a few of the things I had turned up in my studies, but I think much more important to him was finding someone who was deeply interested in banking history and who had some understanding of banking in the United States more than a century ago.

Our conversations took place in the FDIC's offices, then located in the National Press Building, because Bray was no longer at the Federal Reserve. The conversations were usually several hours long, but there were not very many such meetings – I would guess about four. For me they were unforgettable. As Bray would lay the groundwork for an issue or incident about which he was writing, he would speak almost as if he had just talked a bit earlier with some of the persons he would be writing about – say, Nicholas Biddle, President of the Second Bank, or Roger Taney, President Jackson's Secretary of the Treasury – usually as if he had just come from a meeting with them. In fact, as we discussed it, it was almost as if the various personnel involved in a particular incident were present in the shadows of my office. When our sessions ended, usually long past dinnertime, I had to remind myself that it was really 1953 and not 120 years earlier, so fascinating was Bray's "firsthand" account of the matter discussed.

Bray left Washington to take up residence in Italy in order to finish his book, although we did stay in touch because he occasionally had questions of fact that were difficult for him to check, but no problem for me. Several years after the book appeared, in 1958, it received the Pulitzer Prize for History and is certainly one of the best histories I have ever read.

There is another point that I should make here. In recent years, I have begun to wonder about the possibility of a replay of the "Bank War" in the not too distant future. The issue triggering it could be anything. The problem stems from the status of the central bank (now the Federal Reserve), which is often described as "independent within government," a definition usually attributed to William McChesney Martin, a long-time Chairman of the Board of Governors from 1951 to 1970.

The nature of the problem is best understood by noting that the Constitution of the United States makes no provision for a central bank. The reason was the bitter division in our nation's infancy between pro-bank and anti-bank forces. Alexander Hamilton was one of the pro-bank forces who regarded banks as essential, while Thomas Jefferson was one of the anti-bank forces who regarded banks and bankers as evil. It was thought wise by those drafting the Constitution to be silent on banking lest the Constitution be rejected by some of the states.

Today's central bank was established in 1913 and during its first 20 years it had a difficult time. As I described earlier, it is now generally agreed that the catastrophic depression of 1930-33 need never have occurred except for the fact that the Federal Reserve was unable or unwilling to perform as the central bank. Accordingly, the Banking Act of 1935 made significant improvements in the structure and responsibility of the central bank, such that more power was given to the Board of Governors and the Chairman, and there was no question any longer that the Federal Reserve was a federal government institution, notwithstanding any lingering indicia of private ownership. But this still left a great many uncertainties that have never been resolved. For example, to whom does the Federal Reserve report or from whom does it take orders? The answer, apparently, is no one. The independence of the central bank is deemed to be an all-important objective. What limits are there to the activities in which it can engage? Presumably this is decided in the first instance – and usually the last – by the Board of Governors of the Fed itself on the basis of what it believes is needed for it to carry out its central banking responsibilities. How is it financed? Not by the federal government, but by the Federal Reserve itself. Through its money-creating powers, the Fed can assemble on its balance sheet, at virtually no cost to itself, all of the earning assets that the Federal Reserve System needs to obtain a handsome income. Indeed, each year the federal treasury is given, as a kind of a gift from this independent agency, the income that the Fed has decided it does not need.

Arthur F. Burns, a former Chairman of the Board of Governors, is reputed to have claimed that the Federal Reserve is the fourth branch of government. As a matter of fact, this assertion seems quite reasonable when one looks at the government's structure. The only problem is that the Constitution establishes some boundaries for the functions of the other three branches of government – the executive, legislative and judicial – but there are no important restrictions on the Federal Reserve.

A Deep-Seated Resentment. Earlier I had mentioned that Professor Cargill of the University of Nevada had identified several reasons that, in his view, accounted for the long silence that greeted Clark Warburton's articles. One that Cargill suggested was a reluctance to tangle with Clark on certain issues because, "his (Clark's) writing and method of argument often turned his typewriter into a flame-thrower." I saw something like this happen on several occasions, and I still recall one particularly dramatic scene.

In the 1950s, Sen. Paul Douglas (D-Ill.) had the habit of submitting questionnaires to each of the three federal banking agencies raising questions about policies and problems. The questions were usually identical for all three agencies, and I am sure it was no secret that the staffs of the agencies checked among themselves to see whether there were any major differences in their answers that should be explained. One such meeting was held at the FDIC, hosted by Clark Warburton. I was the only other economist from the FDIC present, but the head of our statistical section was probably there also.

As I recall, we had two or three persons from the Federal Reserve and one or two from the Office of the Comptroller of the Currency. The meeting, similar to others I had attended, was friendly and no serious problems with the answers arose. However, just as the group was preparing to break up a serious issue arose, quite by accident. For some reason discussion had drifted into the question of who at the Federal Reserve was responsible for its decision in the summer of 1932 to abandon the recently accelerated program of purchasing Treasury securities in order to increase bank reserves. Congress was desperate for any action to increase the money supply and was insisting on this, but the Federal Reserve's Open Market Committee was opposed. However, the Open Market Committee finally agreed to permit such purchases, presumably fearful of more drastic action by Congress. The larger purchases started in April and were just beginning to show positive results, but Congress adjourned in July. As soon as Congress went home, the Fed drastically reduced the purchases, and this in turn set in motion the final drastic stage of the crisis, resulting in something like 4,000 more bank failures in the following year and the declaration by the new President of a national holiday, closing all banks in March 1933.

Clark became quite agitated during this discussion, but said very little. I knew he was upset because when he was unhappy with the course of a meeting he would carefully, almost fussily, align all of his documents so that they made a very neat pile, in effect signaling that he was about to leave. On this occasion he could not wait, even as the host. He stood up, clutching his papers to his chest, and said that there was no question that whoever was responsible for that decision at the Fed was someone who was either immensely stupid or the agent of a foreign government. Then Clark walked out, only pausing as he opened the door to deliver his parting shot: "And I can assure you that the people in charge of monetary policy at the Board of Governors are not stupid." The door then closed behind him.

Needless to say, the meeting was over. In considering whether to tell this story, it occurred to me that we had met when Sen. Joseph McCarthy (R-Wis.) was prominently in the news, and that some readers might assume that Clark was a McCarthyite. At the time this never occurred to me because I knew, as I think everyone else did, that Clark was a conventional Washington liberal who initially was mildly worried about the election of President Eisenhower because of his fear that the new President would be ultraconservative. This, of course, turned out not to be the case. For me, it was simply another indication of Clark's passionate belief – and I think the word "passionate" is appropriate here – in the correctness of his positions in his chosen field. For Clark, the banking crisis and the associated 10-year depression of the 1930s was a terrible tragedy, both human and economic, that could easily have been prevented. He was not alone in this belief. The consequences of the Fed's not taking action were so horrendous in Clark's view that he simply reached for the most extreme illustration he could think of: a deliberate attack on the United States.

Our Last Meeting. When someone asked me about the last time I had seen Clark Warburton. I wasn't sure at first, but as I thought about it, an incident in the early 1970s came back to me. Most likely it was the last time I saw him, but it was certainly the one that I recall most vividly. It was at the final session of a conference hosted by the FDIC's Research Division for about 50 to 75 economists.

I do not recall now the specific subject of the conference or why I was even present. I assume I was simply one of the invited guests. Ever since I left the FDIC, I had maintained a relationship with the agency – nothing formal, but of the "old school tie" nature. What I do recall quite clearly is the final session and the remarks made by the Chief of the Research Division, Paul M. Horvitz.

Paul's comments were quite brief. He began by stating that in his opinion the FDIC's Research Division had produced, since it was organized in 1934, more significant studies and analyses of monetary policy than the Federal Reserve. He said that Clark Warburton had been almost solely responsible for the Division's record in this respect, noting that Clark had been a senior economist for 32 years beginning in 1934. Then Paul noted that Clark was present this day and introduced him. Almost as if it had been scheduled, the entire audience stood up and clapped long and enthusiastically. It was the kind of tribute that Clark was not accustomed to receiving, and I think it touched him deeply. I had not known that he was going to be present, and I must confess that as I listened to the applause I felt a bit of moisture in my eyes.

Over the last few years, one of the surprising things that I found while spending more time than usual at the FDIC because of this book is that there is not the slightest indication that one of the great pioneers in monetary economics had been on the staff of the FDIC for about 32 years. I think I became aware of this when I asked whether Clark had left any papers because, if so, I would like to see them. But I was told that this treasure trove for scholarly research had been placed by Clark's family with the library of George Mason University in Fairfax, Va.

I was not surprised at this because both inside and outside the FDIC, Clark was indeed a "one-man show." I have no idea whether the FDIC had given Clark the opportunity to store his papers with the Corporation, but if he had been invited to do that, I doubt it would have accepted. Significantly, Clark Warburton is included only twice in the bibliography of the FDIC's own publication *FDIC, the First Fifty Years (1933-1983)*. Moreover, in each instance he is listed only as an author or co-author of histories of early state deposit insurance systems. Numerous other publications dealing with bank failures (such as the Friedman-Schwartz history) are represented. It may seem odd, but I doubt seriously that whoever put together the FDIC's bibliography was aware of Clark's "other life." Still, it is a fact that the spark that ignited Clark's interest in bank failures – the thing that resulted eventually in giving him the title of "Pioneer Monetarist" – was his appreciation of the importance to the FDIC of having a better understanding of the causes of bank failures, including those causes traceable to poor monetary policies.

All of which prompts a small suggestion. A time-tested way of keeping alive interest in a famous scholar's work is an annual dinner in his or her honor, with a prestigious speaker, an audience of prominent and knowledgeable people, and wide distribution of copies of the speech. Such a program, particularly if put together by the FDIC's Division of Research, and with full support from the Chairman and the members of the FDIC Board, could well attract significant interest nationally. The theme would be the same on all occasions: a critical, independent assessment of the FDIC's contribution to economic and monetary stability – past, present or future. It is this kind of thing that would enhance the FDIC's reputation in public policy circles.

Section II
Trade Association Years

This Section deals with events during the 1960s, a particularly interesting time for banking. It does so against a background of the Great Depression that lasted through the decade of the 1930s, then by the problem of financing World War II in the 1940s, and the conviction that seemingly gripped the entire nation during the 1950s that the closing of the war plants would return the nation to the pre-war depression. Many will recall that the early 1930s were the only time in the nation's history that the President of the United States had to order that all banks be closed – those chartered by the states as well as the federal government and those that were or were not members of the Federal Reserve System.

President Roosevelt's action in 1933 brought an end to a banking system that for more than three years had been starved of liquidity. It finally imploded on that bleak Monday of March 6, 1933, when none of the banks were permitted to open. Not surprisingly, when a week or so later the banks were permitted to reopen, many were not able to do so immediately, and others never made it at all. Thus, a few thousand more banks became casualties, meaning that when added to the other bank failures during the four years beginning in 1930, a grand total of about 10,000 banks had perished.

The Great Depression was distinguished for many things, but perhaps most notably its after-effects. Government officials or others who track periods of depression and prosperity pay close attention to turning points as, for example, the decision that enough good news had finally appeared near the end of 1933 to indicate that this too was a turning point. The trouble was that virtually no one at that time would have recognized it as such. In 1939, the year in which World War II started, the national unemployment rate was still an enormous 17.2 percent. The war economy that ensued even before the United States entered World War II in late

1941 immediately ended the unemployment problem, but did little to bring prosperity to the banks. By 1945, according to Professor Benjamin J. Klebaner in his 1974 volume *Commercial Banking in the United States: A History*, U.S. government securities owned by banks were over three and a half times the amount of their loans. Observers, he said, "doubted whether banks would resume their commercial lending function in the postwar period."

There was another impediment to full recovery of the commercial banking industry. Beginning in 1934 the Federal Reserve was no longer free to reach independent decisions on monetary policy without first contacting the Treasury. This was because of the astonishing refusal by the Federal Reserve to deal with the banking crisis in the early 1930s. The situation became even tighter for the Fed once the war began, when the Federal Reserve was required to support the Treasury policy of financing the war at the lowest possible interest cost. Banks ended up with a heavy concentration of Treasury securities. President Truman made it impossible for the Fed to regain its independence until March 4, 1951, when an "accord" with the Treasury was finally reached. Even then, the Federal Reserve had to move cautiously because of the President's strong support for the Treasury position.

The chapters in Section II differ quite a bit, each from the others, but all reflect the belief that the business of commercial banking was likely to be conducted in a setting that had favorable growth and earnings possibilities. The times slowly reflected an increasing optimism throughout the banking industry, something that had not been in large supply during the three preceding decades.

Chapter Five – "The American Bankers Association" – placed its major emphasis on strengthening the dual banking system. The campaign began with ABA's "Symposium on Economic Growth," held on the same day but 100 years later than the date on which the dual system was created (February 25, 1863). The keynote address was made by President Kennedy, who also took questions from the audience of more than 300 of the top leaders in finance, business, agriculture, labor and the academic community. The dual banking theme was expanded and continued in the ABA's annual convention about seven months later. ABA President Archie K. Davis subsequently led, personally, a year-long campaign involving a series of regional and national conferences, working with the states to upgrade the nation's dual banking system.

Chapter Six is titled "An Intervening Episode: My Quest for the FDIC Chairmanship." It deals with the active contest by persons contending for the Presidential appointment to eventually become Chairman of the Federal Deposit Insurance Corporation. I was a central figure in that contest.

Chapter Seven – "The Saxon Revolution and its Aftermath" – describes the effort by James J. Saxon, the new Comptroller of the Currency, to change, in a number of substantial ways, the nature of government regulation of banks in order to bring about a far more competitive banking system. He also sought to eliminate depression-induced limitations on banking. This campaign was conducted vigorously and, many have argued, brilliantly by Saxon. I was one who found no difficulty in terming his campaign "The Saxon Revolution."

Chapter Five
The American Bankers Association

Early in 1960 I received an unsolicited call from an official at the American Bankers Association (ABA), asking if I would be interested in joining that organization as the Secretary of its Research Committee (essentially the Committee's manager). This message came at a time when I had become quite restive at the FDIC. I was beginning to wonder whether, professionally, I was in the proper place at a time when the "Great Depression" was finally beginning to show signs of fading away. I had made no plans, so the telephone call from the ABA literally came out of the blue. Its tone, I thought, was that of an offer with a few details yet to be discussed, rather than an inquiry indicating that ABA was interviewing persons to fill the position of Secretary of its Research Committee. A brief conversation made it clear that my first reaction – that it was, in fact, an offer – was correct.

My restiveness was due to an increasing feeling on my part that the FDIC was not likely to offer very much in the way of challenging work or interesting new assignments. This was not because there was no such work to be done, but rather because there was little that would excite my particular interests or my training. Banking is a business almost entirely in private hands, but one that is still thoroughly regulated by government. I have always found that the most interesting and important issues arose because of the interplay between the private and public interests involved. Also, I must confess to my long-term fascination with economic history.

The FDIC at that time was still following a deliberate policy of avoiding involvement in almost any significant controversy involving banking. An exception was the management of the government's guarantee of deposits held by failing banks – a subject that the Corporation properly regarded as special to it. Thus, unless a banking issue was one of direct and special importance to the FDIC, the practice of the Corporation was to avoid taking a position (or testifying if it was a legislative matter). Another tactic was to take a mild position, but arranging that the FDIC's testimony would appear late in the process, thus usually avoiding questioning.

I never discussed this policy with senior FDIC officials when I was putting together speeches or testimony for one or the other of the directors, but it did seem to be a reasonable and, as it turned out, effective policy in the FDIC's early years. In the debates in the 1930s over deposit insurance legislation, opponents constantly harped on the argument that government protection of depositors in failed banks had almost always been unsuccessful. Accordingly, top management of the FDIC made sure that the No. 1 objective, particularly in the very early years, was the survival of the agency, even if this meant less generous treatment of depositors of failed banks. It was clear that the FDIC intended to be around for a while. This, of course, left a question of how long this protective strategy had to be continued since it was still in effect as late as the 1960s, and I saw few signs of any intention of changing it.

It would not be easy for me to leave the FDIC. There was no question in my mind that the FDIC was, and I believe still is, one of the finest agencies in Washington in terms of its achievements and professionalism. It was no mean accomplishment to provide supervision for the largest portion of the banking system, when measured by the number of institutions, and to manage the government's deposit insurance commitment. But I must add that the prospect of spending much time doing research on, or speaking about, or defending (or attacking) the size of the FDIC's deposit insurance fund held no attraction for me. I have always believed that the amount of time and study that inevitably went into analyzing the "insurance" commitment was a drag on the FDIC, however much that appealed to academics and others who found it a great sandbox in which to play. After all, no matter how dressed up, it was nothing more than a guarantee by the federal government. Sadly, keeping the FDIC saddled with the government's commitment to depositors in failed banks had the effect of keeping the FDIC from becoming a major player among the federal financial agencies.

More than a few prestigious studies, as early as the 1930s, have suggested that the FDIC's supervisory authority should be expanded to include all state banks, even those that were state-chartered but members of the Federal Reserve System. Some even went further, pointing out that "deposit insurance" could be handled more appropriately by another agency, particularly one not purporting to "insure deposits." I did not sense any interest in such proposals by the FDIC. Thus, it seemed to me that administering the government's guarantee would continue to be an unnecessary distraction from much more important work by the FDIC. It was, in fact, the principal reason that I decided to accept the offer by the ABA.

ABA in 1960-61. I joined the ABA in what can be described as a backward manner. In April 1960, I left the FDIC and went directly to the Greenbrier Hotel in White Sulfur Springs, W.Va., where the ABA was having its most important meeting of senior ABA officers and banker members of ABA divisions, committees and other administrative bodies. I did not, therefore, report first to the New York headquarters of the ABA in order to meet persons with whom or for whom I would be working, nor did I have the opportunity to meet the staff of the Research Committee. As a matter of fact, I was not even certain that I was on the ABA's payroll at the time that I reported for duty, but that must have been taken care of in some way. On balance, I thought it was an awkward and improper way for me to join the ABA.

The explanation was that Erle Cocke, Sr., a Director of the FDIC appointed by President Eisenhower to a six-year term in 1957, wanted it that way. He and I were friendly, and I had done some writing for him during my years at the FDIC. As a matter of fact, in 1963 when I was a candidate for appointment to the FDIC's Board of Directors, Cocke called me (by that time he had become the Chairman of the FDIC) to say that he had given the President (or more likely, one of the President's senior staff) his recommendation that I should be appointed to the FDIC Board, but that he had also recommended only one other individual for the same position. Cocke said that the latter was a confidential matter and he could not mention the name of the other person to me. When it came to Washington appointments, Erle Cocke, Sr., never risked being on the losing side.

In any event, in 1960 Cocke insisted that I be sent to the ABA's Spring Meeting, scheduled for about mid-April at the Greenbrier Hotel. He believed, and had reason for thinking so, that only very senior staff members were eligible to participate in the meeting. Possibly I would be invited the next year, in 1961, but that was not a certainty. Having been invited to this meeting, where it would quickly be known that the Chairman of the Board of the FDIC had recommended the invitation would be a quite effective move. This fact would be known among the other senior staff and bankers. Cocke was, of course, quite confident of this because in 1956, before he was nominated by President Eisenhower to be a member of the FDIC Board, he had been the banker President of the American Bankers Association.

Chairman Cocke called me to his office at the FDIC to explain his reasoning for what he was doing. As I was sitting there, he called a top official at the FDIC to take care of this. It was not a short conversation, because of the obvious objections brought forth by the FDIC to this strange way of intervening on behalf of a brand new hire of a private organization. However, Cocke was not a man who was easily dissuaded from carrying out his particular plans, and he was not in this case. The conversation ended with his "Thank you very much, please take care of this quickly" or something like that.

So a few days later I found myself with a package of credentials in hand authorizing me to be transported by railroad to the Greenbrier. The hotel was indeed owned by the railroad. The train's first-class cars for bankers and ABA senior staff were unloaded only at the Greenbrier, probably having started in Boston with stops in New York, Washington and Virginia. I had a few friends among the bankers and staff so I was introduced around with no problems. The special cars were staffed entirely by Greenbrier waiters and porters, some of whom were known to the attendees, making it a festive occasion. We arrived at the Greenbrier at about 5 a.m., but only the special cars were dropped off at the hotel so that passengers could continue to sleep or have a very early breakfast. All in all, it was an interesting way of finding yourself introduced to your new employer, a way that has since disappeared with the Greenbrier now accessible by air and better roads.

The ABA was probably the nation's oldest banker association and certainly the largest, founded in 1875 by a prominent New York City banker, George S. Coe, President of the American Exchange National Bank. Coe is now largely forgotten, but history buffs might find interesting an article describing his many banking achievements, written by Professor Fritz Redlich of Harvard University. It appears as an appendix to Redlich's towering history of U.S. banking. Coe is the only banker so honored among the many hundreds of bankers described in that history.

Whether measured by number of banks or volume of bank assets, ABA's membership in 1951, at the time I joined the FDIC, was, as I recollect, comfortably close to 98 percent of the banking industry. I assume it was about at the same level in 1960. Members consisted almost entirely of institutions generally termed "commercial banks," which meant that they provided demand deposit facilities for the general public. In 1960, there were more than 14,000 such commercial banks, as well as a much smaller number of mutual savings banks (several of them quite large) included in the ABA membership. Mutual savings banks (much less numerous than savings and loan associations) were found almost entirely in New England and the Middle Atlantic states.

No other banker association sought to embrace all banks. Every state probably had at least one association for banks operating just in that state, with such associations generally working closely with the ABA. The ABA had virtually all banks as members at that time, regardless of the size or nature of activity. Other national associations tended to seek out banks with a particular business focus, such as agriculture, or they stressed size characteristics. Several of these size-oriented associations were becoming quite powerful. The Independent Bankers Association (later titled the Independent Community Bankers of America) consisted of smaller banks (in 1960 there were more than 12,000 banks with less than $25 million in deposits), whereas the Association of Reserve City Bankers (now titled the Financial Services Roundtable) consisted of quite large banks. In 1960, it was not unusual for a bank to have two, three or even four association memberships, and almost always one of these included the ABA.

The American Bankers Association in the 1960s had four major divisions (national bank, state bank, trust and savings) involved primarily in broad policy matters, along with approximately 30 operating committees, such as the Banking Research Committee, and a wide variety of banker education facilities topped by the Stonier Graduate School of Banking. Banker education has always been an important association activity because of the relative ease with which newcomers could enter banking under our unique "free banking" laws. In all, the number of bankers participating in the administration of the ABA exceeded well over 500 persons, while the ABA's senior staff in 1960 totaled about 75, as I recall. However, participation by bankers in educational activities supported by ABA, much of it voluntary, was also of major importance.

Readers may recall that my entrance into government's bank regulatory world was not without unexpected difficulty. The same was true of this much more recent attempt to enter the bankers' world, courtesy of the American Bankers Association. My problem this time was that I made a serious mistake in failing to do a proper "due diligence" procedure with respect to the offer I had received from the ABA. The ABA, incidentally, also erred in assuming that I would be interested in landing the position it had in mind, but my error was worse.

I had assumed, without making proper inquiry, that my committee would have an important role to play when it came to shaping ABA policies or assisting in developing them. This did not turn out to be the case. Other ABA committees had those responsibilities whereas the Research Committee, as I understood it, was then deeply involved in obtaining and making available, both to bankers and to other ABA committees, accurate and useful data. My Committee, I was told, produced regular publications of data that were useful to some members, and it also advised other ABA committees on the kinds of data that would be most useful to them. While all of this was quite important, it was something in which I had no great interest and, although I hesitate to admit it, not very much skill either.

My first reaction, after concluding that I had indeed made a major mistake was to explore the possibility of expanding the scope of the Research

Committee's responsibilities, adding analyses of policy proposals or banking issues facing the ABA, a responsibility that I had assumed, perhaps incorrectly, had been included in the work of the Research Committee in earlier years. I spent some time over a period of three or four months in 1960 testing the waters about the proposal I had just mentioned and found, somewhat to my surprise, a significant element of support for such an expansion, both from members of the Research Committee and other persons I consulted informally. However, it seemed to me that to be successful in adding to the specific responsibilities of the Research Committee might be a fairly long job. Moreover, when I examined the ABA's 1960-61 "Official List," I noted that the ABA already had a number of committees that were dealing in one fashion or another with federal legislation. Two of these committees consisted of, in one instance, about 50 banker members, while the other committee had about 60 banker members. I wondered how much could really be done by such large committees. In any event, I wanted to note the existence of other committees in the field, not only the two I just mentioned, but others as well.

One committee in particular interested me. It was ABA's prestigious Economic Policy Committee. This committee in 1960-61 was chaired by Jesse W. Tapp, Chairman of the Board of Bank of America, and had 12 bank members, one of whom was an official of a mutual savings bank. The other members consisted almost entirely of prominent bankers from quite large banks scattered about the country. Virtually all were titled Chairman or President of their respective banking organizations. I suppose that all American Bankers Association committees were of equal importance but, as the saying goes, some are far more equal than others. This was certainly the case with the Economic Policy Committee.

There was a new committee named the Committee for Economic Growth Without Inflation. It may have been intended to reflect some of the luster that the new U.S. President, John F. Kennedy, was preaching. In any event, it had a strange history. Its Chairman was Casimir A. Sienkiewicz, the respected President of the Central-Penn National Bank in Philadelphia, Pa. All but one of its members, including the Chairman, were also members of the Economic Policy Committee. The sixth member was Roy L. Reierson, a highly regarded economist who was a Senior Vice President at Bankers Trust Company of New York. However, this committee did have an impressive roster of advisors, whereas at the time the Economic Policy Committee had none. In fact, the new committee had three of the top economists in the United States: Gottfried Haberler of Harvard, Fritz Machlup of Princeton and Paul W. McCracken of the University of Michigan.

A comparison with my committee members suggests the magnitude of the task if I were seeking to find a special place for the Research Committee. In 1960, the Research Committee had 13 banker members who were all Vice Presidents at their institutions. Five had "And Economist" tacked on to their title, while six others probably were economists as well, but were not so recognized in their official titles. We had only one senior executive from a large bank, Louis B. Lundborg, Executive Vice President of the Bank of America, as well as an official representing the Savings Bank Association of Massachusetts. The banks represented on my committee tended to be of larger size because it was usually only larger banks that designated the position of economist.

I thought it likely that the prior Secretary had followed a policy of selecting economists for membership, with a healthy mixture of differing views and ages. As a group, I was quite impressed with the Research Committee. On the basis of my first three meetings with the committee, I thought it quite likely that its deliberations would be much livelier and a lot more fun than those of the Economic Policy Committee. However, it would take a great deal of time and effort to change my committee to create better membership balance, preserving the exuberance of some of the members and, at the same time, have a better platform for serious issues. So even though the idea of slowly but carefully reforming the committee would be a tempting challenge, I concluded that I simply did not have enough time.

A note on the fate of the new Growth Without Inflation Committee. It had a short life. After 1960, which I think was probably its organizational year, it added several new members in 1961, making several excellent selections of well-known bankers from large institutions who were not concurrently serving on the Economic Policy Committee. It also retained most of the initial members who had an overlap with the Economic Policy Committee. Then in 1962, the new committee disappeared. My guess – and I must emphasize "guess" because I had moved on to other matters – was that its mistake had been to move too rapidly to occupy a part of the turf of the Economic Policy Committee.

Then a few years later, I came across a copy of the ABA's "Official List" for 1965-66. I noticed that the Economic Policy Committee had been substantially increased in size, thus becoming less "special," though still continuing its policy of drawing members almost entirely from top officials of large banks. And I also found that my old Research Committee had a new title – Banking and Financial Research Committee – suggesting a good mixture of economists and bankers from various size groups. It had an important link with the Economic Policy Committee – its Secretary, Thomas R. Atkinson, also serving as the Secretary of the Economic Policy

Committee. Atkinson was an outstanding economist in his own right. I was delighted, of course, but I also had to note that it required about five years, as I had expected, to reach this point.

Returning now to 1960, I had a difficult choice to make. I concluded that I should resign from the American Bankers Association, thanking Merle E. Selecman, ABA's Executive Manager, for the opportunity to handle a most interesting position, although not mentioning why I thought it could be made so. Instead, I stressed the importance that I attached to completing the requirements for my law degree (to add to my doctorate in economics). I had been a registered student, primarily in night school, for almost 10 years at George Washington University Law School in Washington, D.C. Recently the Dean arranged to meet with a group of long-time students of which I was one (but not the record holder) who had more than enough credits to graduate, but lacked certain required courses and gave no indication of any interest in graduating. He made it clear that we had only one year (two terms) to complete our work and graduate. I had only a few ignored courses to take such as "torts."

As for the timing of my ABA departure, I had written Selecman that it was entirely up to him. However, if he wanted me to complete some of the work I had promised members of my committee at our meeting the previous fall, I could do it but could not stay beyond the end of April 1961. In any event, I never received an answer from Selecman, even though I knew from a conversation with his secretary that my resignation was sitting on his desk. Frankly, I was a little irritated, although I soon dropped this attitude when it became apparent that the people in charge of the ABA had more pressing things to do than deal with a routine resignation. Also, it occurred to me that the ABA was reacting to the same environmental changes facing the rest of the banking industry in the post-war era, and that decisions had to be made on the opportunities and the problems that lay ahead.

Charlie Walker and the "New" ABA. Unbeknownst to me, and I assume to many others as well, an important part of the senior management group had been planning for fundamental change, not in the size or committee structure of the ABA but instead in its management. As a relative newcomer, I had no idea how long or how deeply this current had been running. In any event, I was not very interested because I had already solved my problem. However, since there had been no reply to my letter of resignation, I assumed that the part saying that I must leave by the end of April 1961 was in play and that any reaction to my letter would await Selecman's successor. Since no one seemed to be aware of my resignation, I decided to do nothing further and just wait to see what might develop.

The 1961 ABA Spring Meeting was likely to be quite unusual and remembered for many years. The association had not yet completed its restructuring work. We were all given to understand that a few last points would be settled very soon. As I said earlier, the Spring Meeting of the ABA was the most important of the large meetings, more important even than the Annual Convention in the fall. The Annual Convention, which sometimes attracted more than 10,000 people, was typically not much more than a gigantic party. In addition to partying, the attendees approved certain matters on which agreement had been reached at an earlier date. In fact, most of these decisions had been made at the Spring Meeting in the preceding April. As I think about it 50 years later, the change in ABA's management was carried off rather smoothly, suggesting that some careful thought and planning had gone into this matter. The only awkwardness was the fact that a few items were left until the first day of the Spring Meeting, but otherwise the transition was handled, I thought, quite well given the circumstances.

The newly appointed Executive Manager was Dr. Charls E. Walker, a professor at the University of Texas who also had spent some time, I believe, at the Federal Reserve Bank of Dallas. I knew him slightly because we both had attended, over the years, several of the same sessions at annual conventions of the American Economic Association. So we were on a first-name basis, but certainly were not close acquaintances. In fact, I was quite surprised when, a day or two after returning to New York and while I was putting my papers in order for my successor (and wondering if anyone would even notice that I would be gone very soon), Charlie called, asking if we could discuss my resignation letter that he had just seen for the first time.

Initially, I did not expect very much from meeting with Charlie, other than perhaps a pleasant "goodbye." He surprised me, however, by taking the opportunity to describe some of his plans for handling his new ABA position. I assumed he was doing the same thing with other acquaintances who were familiar with ABA – after all, Charlie had been at ABA only a week or so – and he would likely look for reactions to his ideas from people who were familiar with how ABA operated, but who were not deeply involved in the organization itself. Actually, he and I had several meetings, and I then began to wonder if he had another motive, which was to see if I would be more interested in a different position than that of Secretary of the Research Committee. As it turned out, he was. I soon withdrew my resignation letter at Charlie's request, as I will describe later. In any event, I thought it might be of some interest to describe my impressions drawn from these few conversations with Charlie in those opening days of his taking over.

I came away from our first discussion with two quite strong impressions. First, Charlie had come to ABA with the clear intention of being its Chief

Executive Officer. To be sure, this was not what the ABA charter said. That document specified that the elected banker president each year became, at the same time, the ABA's Chief Executive Officer. Still, everyone at the ABA realized that it had been Selecman, as ABA's Executive Manager (with the additional title of Executive Vice President) who, in fact, essentially filled the CEO position, as had some of his predecessors. It was Selecman's position that Charlie was assuming. I was told that it had always been a joke among ABA staff members that those banker presidents with great plans for changing or influencing ABA policy rarely got the opportunity to do so because by the time they had fulfilled their Presidential speech schedule, their year as President was near its end.

Charlie Walker planned to be the CEO of the organization representing virtually all banks in the United States – and to be recognized as such. To be sure, the CEOs of some prominent banks would at times receive public attention for a variety of reasons, but an industry with 14,000 banks had to have a recognized leader on certain major policy issues, and Charlie Walker intended to be that person. Charlie, of course, never made such a suggestion, or anything like it, in our conversations. It was simply an impression of mine, and one that I quietly welcomed. (More recently, the ABA adopted a realistic management structure, with a banker elected as Chairman for one-year and a President and CEO appointed by the Board of Directors).

The second impression I received was that Charlie recognized that ABA no longer walked with a heavy tread among other major industry representatives. This diminution of stature could not be blamed on the banking industry entirely, but instead resulted from a number of major developments that occurred in previous decades, several beyond banking's control. One was the Federal Reserve's role in the Great Depression. The collapse of the banking system then was not beyond the control of the Federal Reserve. In fact, it was one of the historic responsibilities of the central bank. But it was a responsibility that the Federal Reserve failed to accept, to the astonishment of, among many others, the President of the United States, Herbert Hoover. The ABA, and banking generally, had gone through a horrendous experience in 1932-33, when it became the only industry in the nation that had ever been shut down completely by a Presidential directive (by President Roosevelt in March 1933). A long economic depression followed, which did not really end until 1939-40. This produced the coldest judgment I have ever encountered in any discussion of Federal Reserve policy. In his excellent history of the Federal Reserve, Dr. Allan H. Meltzer wrote (in Volume I, with a Forward by Alan Greenspan) that in 1930-33:

The Federal Reserve had been indecisive and incompetent as the banking problem became a crisis. The [Federal Reserve] Board now took a back seat. The Treasury and the new President [Mr. Roosevelt] made the policy decisions.

That back seat lasted for the next 20 years.

However, one Federal Reserve blunder that apparently escaped review was the decision to double required bank reserves in 1936-37. The Fed's assumption was that this would have little or no effect on the banks themselves since they already held excess reserves roughly equal to required reserves. Presumably the thought was that getting rid of excess reserves would make banks quite sensitive to later anti-inflationary actions. As a matter of fact, the Fed's action immediately touched off the third most severe recession since World War I. For example, the unemployment rate reached almost 20 percent of the labor force, not much below its horrendous high of 25 percent in 1933. According to Meltzer, it was "no wonder that many feared that the 1930-33 disaster had returned."

Then came the wartime subordination of the Federal Reserve to the Treasury, which brought Treasury's tight regulation of interest rates and bond prices. Finally, in the late 1940s and early 1950s, there emerged a widespread belief among large numbers of people, including many bankers, that a great postwar depression was a certainty. This turned out, fortunately, to be wrong. The Federal Reserve finally began to regain its independence in the famous Treasury-Federal Reserve Accord in March 1951. However, as Meltzer pointed out in his summary of the first 37 years of the Fed's existence, when William McChesney Martin, Jr. became Chairman of the Federal Reserve Board, "one of his tasks was to establish the independence of the Federal Reserve System from the executive branch, particularly the Treasury."

There was, however, another factor for which the ABA could only blame itself. Deposit insurance was tremendously popular. It was regarded as the only possible savior of the great number of small banks. ABA was not only a leading opponent of the enabling legislation in the early 1930s, but it also persisted in its efforts until after the legislation had passed by both houses, by attempting to persuade President Roosevelt to veto the measure. Even though Mr. Roosevelt was as much opposed to deposit insurance as the ABA, he found that he could not fight it. In the end, he focused simply on limiting the amount that an individual bank depositor could recover from the FDIC ($2,500) and then "leaked" to the press a story that he favored the idea of deposit insurance under the new law. The President's new approach toward this legislation infuriated those in Congress who had fought the great battle for adequate deposit insurance coverage over Mr. Roosevelt's quiet but powerful opposition. Ironically, Mr. Roosevelt is the President who is now recognized most often as the person who brought deposit insurance to the United States.

By the 1960s, the future beckoned, particularly to those who had begun to believe that the banking world had, in fact, changed, with bankers facing both great opportunities and serious challenges. Banking could not afford to remain passive in such circumstances and yet for many bankers there seemed to be little desire to do anything except to batten down the hatches and wait for the next problem. I had a strong hunch that Charlie Walker believed the times called for vigorous action to restore the political position of the ABA, but he never mentioned this. Still I thought this was particularly likely in view of the fact that the new leader of the national banks, from the government side, was James J. Saxon, the new Comptroller of the Currency. Saxon had begun to obtain a great deal of support for his fight to reduce or eliminate outdated restrictions on national banks.

An early subject Charlie Walker and I discussed was the position of banking research in ABA. It quickly became evident that Charlie wanted to create in ABA a banking and financial research facility that would rival the finest in the United States in terms of ability and independence. He wanted the ABA to model its research activities after those at several of the Federal Reserve Banks that had been attracting favorable attention for the quality and the independence of their work. As I recall, he mentioned in particular the Federal Reserve Bank of St. Louis and others such as the Reserve Banks in Minneapolis, Cleveland and San Francisco. However, these might have occurred in later conversations; I am only certain of the St. Louis Federal Reserve Bank. In any event, Charlie believed that his planned new research department should be located in ABA's New York City office because New York was, arguably at least, the world financial capital.

Almost certainly topping the list of changes sought by those who had engineered the management upheaval in ABA was the creation of a powerful legislative office located in Washington, D.C. To be sure, ABA had maintained a Washington office for many years, but generally it remained thinly staffed. Its major contribution, at least during my short tenure at ABA, involved reporting to the New York office on significant Washington developments. In the 1960s, that would not be enough.

All signs pointed towards a major expansion in the supervision and regulation of banks. Moreover, the changing emphasis of regulation was to place primary reliance on the creation of rules having the force of law, rather than the traditional emphasis on oversight and personal supervision. In a sense, government was reacting to the new needs for supervision that would be generated because the fading influence of the Great Depression was making possible many new activities for banks.

Even the titles of the banks or bank associations now headquartered in or focusing on Washington were beginning to reflect the gradual disappearance of banking as a unique or special business. The word "financial" seemed to be edging out "bank," as in "financial institution." "Community" appeared to be replacing "independent" as the code word for "small." Still, "independent" lingered on, probably because of its historic roots. Originally intended to mean any bank conducting business without a branch office (in 1950, for example, 91 percent of the nation's 14,000 commercial banks had only a single banking office and were known as "unit banks"). "Independent" also was intended to exclude banks owned by multi-bank holding companies. Today, however, unit banks have largely disappeared and multi-bank holding companies are consolidating or merging. What the word "independent" is now intended to convey is not clear – possibly "virtuous."

ABA's success in building a Washington office was remarkable, given that it could not be done simply by moving to Washington those staffers already focusing on Washington developments but located in New York. Actually, ABA had few such people, certainly not enough to build a highly professional staff quickly. Nevertheless the new Executive Manager clearly intended to do so.

The major new appointments to Washington are worth noting not only for the rapidity of appointments but also for their top quality. First, Charles R. McNeill, a U.S. Treasury official, became head of the ABA's Washington office in 1961, rather clearly the No. 2 ABA staff position behind Charlie Walker, who remained in New York. Three other appointments quickly followed, beginning with William T. Heffelfinger as Federal Administrative Advisor and Secretary of the Government Borrowing Committee, at that time a quite powerful committee in the ABA. Bill Heffelfinger spent virtually his entire career at the U.S. Treasury and, upon his retirement, I recall that one of the major Washington newspapers carried a laudatory editorial about Heffelfinger, bemoaning the fact that the government had lost one of its outstanding civil servants. Another appointment at about the same time made John W. Holton ABA's Federal Legislative Counsel and Secretary of the Federal Legislative Committee. Holton had spent many years on the staff of the legendary Rep. Sam Rayburn (D-Tex.), who served as Speaker of the House of Representatives through almost the entire period from 1940 until his retirement in 1961, except for two brief mistakes (as he would have viewed it) when Republicans were in the majority and Rayburn was the House Minority Leader. During the later years of Rayburn's career as Speaker of the House, John Holton served as his chief of staff. Then, adding political balance as well as acknowledged expertise, James E. Smith (who later would serve as Comptroller of the Currency) had been persuaded to leave the staff of Sen. Karl Mundt (R-S.D.) to become Assistant Federal Legislative Counsel of the ABA. The Senator had been a powerful Republican member for many years. I should make it quite clear that I had nothing to do with any of these appointments. The only reason Charlie happened to bring up names was that he was not sure whether he had made the final arrangements yet with one or two of the people and simply did not want me to talk about them, which I, of course, said I would not. Insofar as I was personally concerned, I was greatly impressed with the names he gave me and I must say that, if nothing else, they convinced me that he was taking the high road in building a new legislative department.

My guess is that I became involved in the new Washington office because Charlie Walker was an economist and wanted to have someone with that background on board. He asked if I would agree to withdraw my resignation from ABA. He also offered an additional title: Economic Consultant to the Washington Office. I retained the title I already had, which was Deputy Manager, and would soon be appointed Secretary of the State Bank Division. Charlie suggested that a small support staff would be acceptable, and I immediately persuaded Dr. Edison H. Cramer, the retiring Chief of the FDIC's Research Division, to join me. Because of the movement of the State Bank Division staff to the Washington office, I was able to complete work on my law degree at George Washington University. As for other new staff, I added in addition a professional librarian to set up a new library for the expanded Washington office, and persuaded Harriet S. Scholl to leave the FDIC and become my Administrative Assistant. Among several others, I was happy to bring John Gill aboard. He had just completed his bar examination and was exceedingly helpful. In fact, after a number of years he was named the General Counsel of ABA by Willis Alexander (Walker's successor as Executive Manager when Walker was nominated by President Richard M. Nixon to be Under Secretary of the Treasury, the No. 2 position in that cabinet agency at the time). John had a long and successful career as ABA General Counsel until he retired.

The decade of the 1960s was a busy one for ABA. During much of that time, debate raged over the question of whether bank mergers were properly subject to the nation's antitrust laws, as the Department of Justice continually maintained, or were better regulated by the banking agencies, with the banking agencies and the banking industry generally favoring the latter. The battle ended before the end of the decade, with the position of the Department of Justice prevailing. All the banks got out of this was some additional regulation as both the Department of Justice and the appropriate banking agency were empowered to submit separate opinions on whether the merger in question poses anticompetitive problems.

ABA and the Dual Banking System. There was, however, another issue to come before the ABA in the early 1960s. It involved the dual banking system. It was precipitated by some national bankers who wanted to recognize that the national banking system would celebrate its 100th year on February 25, 1963. The ABA agreed that this would be appropriate. The leader of the national bank group was Ben H. Wooten, Chairman of the Board of the First National Bank of Dallas, Tex. ABA asked Wooten to chair a new Centennial Commission, which he did.

There were some who had reservations about having a special event focused just on national banks. They feared that this might not sit well with bankers operating state-chartered institutions. Such state banks constituted the largest portion of ABA's membership, even though national banks were much larger in average size. Also, this kind of thing might prompt a few students of bank history to note that some supporters of national banking a century ago were quite hopeful that the new system would be so attractive to state-chartered banks that it would rid banking of state banks. Others more than hoped. An attempt by Congress in 1865 to encourage charter conversions by placing a 10 percent tax on banknotes issued by state banks was, in fact, quite effective in persuading a good many state-chartered banks to obtain national charters. Under the new legislation, only national banks could issue banknotes that usually became part of the nation's circulating currency. These notes were backed fully by Treasury bonds. There was a brief fear that state banks might disappear. However, when making loans as early as the 1830s, for example, some banks in the United States in the larger cities had found it much more convenient to credit the demand deposit accounts of borrowers rather than to issue the bank's currency for the amount of the loan. By 1855, historians agree that this practice had become so common that mostly it was only small banks, often in the agricultural sectors of the nation, that were still hoping for new legislation enabling them to issue their own currency. Democrats pledged to make this possible in their various Presidential platforms by including a plank to repeal the 10 percent tax, but even this hope disappeared from Democrat party platforms after 1892 because it was no longer needed. The currency of the United States remained essentially in the hands of national banks (and nowadays with Federal Reserve Banks). Yet one still hears suggestions that state-chartered banks "invented" checking accounts and deposit banking. In one sense they did since they were the only banks in the nation. But the charters were not responsible. The fact is that in most instances, such as this, advances or improvements in banking occur simply because bankers themselves take such actions when they identify cost-effective alternatives. After taking office in 1961, President Kennedy had been making a number of speeches about the need for public debate on the matter of economic growth. The President thought that tax reduction would be the most helpful step, but he wanted to discuss this with major business leaders. Apparently someone in ABA had contacted the President's office and said that the American Bankers Association would like to sponsor a Symposium on Economic Growth. For the audience, ABA would invite the leaders in finance, business, agriculture, labor and the academic community. This was exactly what the President desired, and he accepted the offer. Not only that, President Kennedy agreed to keynote the symposium and take questions from the audience. I do not know who thought of this possibility, which suddenly had become a reality. I contacted more than a few people attempting to discover the person, but I was unsuccessful. Several persons suggested that it had probably come from the J. Walter Thompson Agency, which the ABA had on retainer at that time. This did seem reasonable. On the other hand, my own thought had been that ABA's new Executive Manager, Charlie Walker, must have had a hand in this since the subject clearly called for help from an economist. The Symposium on Economic Growth was a roaring success. It could not have been otherwise, given the fact that President Kennedy was the main attraction and that ABA had assembled an outstanding group of speakers, as well as an audience of top executives from all industries to hear and question the speakers. The President made a strong statement of his case for tax reduction. There were nine speakers for the one-day session, including several prominent economists, and while all speakers attached importance to tax reduction, several made suggestions of which they believed to be of even more importance. The audience of more than 300 was every bit as prominent and interactive as could be desired.

At this point I cannot resist adding a brief description of the part I played in the Symposium. The session itself was held in the Grand Ballroom of Washington's Mayflower Hotel. The Chinese Room adjoins the Grand Ballroom and, on special occasions such as this, serves simply as the entrance for the Ballroom. On that day the Chinese room was occupied by the members of ABA's Centennial Commission, headed by its Chairman, Ben Wooten, and a galaxy of former ABA Presidents who were there to welcome Mr. Kennedy. There would be some brief photo opportunities and then they would escort him into the ballroom. My job was to see that all ABA personnel, other than those having something to do with the welcoming delegation, would be out of the Chinese Room once the President arrived. My counterpart from the hotel was overseeing the distribution of coffee, rolls, donuts and so forth to others in the Chinese room, largely television cameramen and reporters. All persons not necessary in the room were required to be out when the President arrived.

Suddenly it was announced over the loud speaker that the President was arriving in 10 minutes. The hotel's "roll man" and I took care of our respective jobs. Having shooed everyone out who was supposed to be out, we then went to the entry doors just as they were being slammed shut. Then, suddenly, the doors opened and the President walked in.

The cameras and microphones had been turned on the minute the President stepped in, but fortunately the first few scenes never aired. However, some of my friends were among those filming the first 20 to 30 seconds of the President's entry and saw a rather strange sight. There were only two persons in front of the entry door when the President walked in – namely, the gentleman from the hotel and me, with the distinguished banker's welcoming group standing several steps below us and not in the picture. The hotel "roll man," well-dressed in formal attire with black tie, walked up to the President, who had extended his hand thinking he was one of the greeters. But the "roll man" simply welcomed the President to the Mayflower. So the President turned aside for me, the second person to welcome him, except that I didn't. Instead, I sought to direct his attention to the Welcoming Committee, but it came out looking like I was rejecting the President's outstretched hand. Actually, the President took one quick look and immediately knew what had happened. He brushed past me without acknowledging my presence and went directly to the Welcoming Committee. All was well.

Not really, particularly if one had access to those 20 to 30 seconds of film. In the scenes that followed, I can be seen in the back, trying hard to disappear into the ground. For several days afterwards, my so-called friends from ABA delighted in telling me that I had obviously permitted my Republican feelings to show and had refused to shake the hand of the President of the United States. And they had the photographs to prove it! I have yet to forgive them!

The reception given the Symposium on Economic Growth tempted ABA's Public Relations Committee to celebrate another product of the 1863 legislation: the creation of a dual banking system. This was a popular result, evidenced by the fact that by 1963 there were 7,184 banks chartered by individual states compared with 4,615 national banks. The national banks were, on average, larger than the state banks. However, a fear one hundred years ago – that only national banks would survive – had long since disappeared. Inevitably, a film was made of the creation of the new dual banking structure. A book was commissioned and published to emphasize the importance of a dual system. *Financing American Enterprise* by Paul Trescott of Kenyon College was a quite respectable publication, although apparently not a wild bestseller. However, its distribution was nationwide and it told an interesting story. Most impressive was the show put on by ABA's Public Relations Committee in the Washington's Constitution Hall of the Daughters of the American Revolution. I could not be present, to my great regret, because of a personal conflict. However, I had heard a great many complimentary stories about that performance, and recently I was able to persuade Raymond (Skip) Cheseldine, then the Executive Secretary of ABA's Centennial Commission (and later head of the Bank Marketing Association), to give me his first-hand impressions of what happened that evening. It follows, as I received it from him:

> To:Carter
> From:Ray Cheseldine, ABA
>
> Last week's phone conversation regarding ABA in the period 1961-63 sent my mind tumbling like clothes in the drier. So many memories, so many memories lost. What follows is a cascade of recollections with no claim to accuracy. Forty-plus years seem to have scrambled truths and warped events.
>
> One day, probably in late 1961 or very early 1962 at our 39th and Park offices in New York, I was summoned by Ruth Wimett to the new boss's corner digs. I was sure I was in hot water and in one respect I was. Charlie [Walker, ABA's Executive Manager] put me somewhat at ease and then began to describe a grand event, an historic future industry celebration which I would be a part of – The Centennial of the Dual Banking System 1863 – 1963. I trembled in anticipation and nearly scorched into orbit!
>
> Even at my tender age, I could detect that Charlie . . . had to pin it on somebody so I jumped into the barrel like a good soldier. There was an ever so faint hint of future rewards and glory – if – I would accept the assignment as Executive Director, The Banking Centennial. Like all good soldiers, I immediately made an estimate of the situation, determined what the mission was, calculated the strength of opposing forces and inventoried friendly assets. That took about 10 minutes. I had met the enemy and he was us.

Originally, this was to be a National Bank Division celebration tied to the signing of the National Currency Act of 1863. . . The State Bank Division felt left out and they weren't about to sit around the wall while the National Bank folks danced. Thus, the great celebration morphed into a celebration of the establishment of the Dual Banking System. The Commission, whose members were known to you, was formed.

A word about J. Walter Thompson. They had been ABA's public relations consultants well before I arrived. Bob Howard was their handler. Gradually, I inherited responsibility for the relationship. Occupying several floors in the Graybar building adjacent to Grand Central Station, it was always a treat to meet in their offices. They "did things up brown," whatever that meant. You were anticipated and treated like royalty the moment you stepped off the elevator. . .

The kick-off event, as you will, of course, remember, was the Symposium in February 1963 in D.C. at the Mayflower Hotel with President Kennedy as the keynoter. Wasn't it titled – A Symposium on Economic Growth Without Inflation, or some such? You were involved so I don't have to describe it. To me it was very impressive. . .

You asked what came between the February opening gun and Abe Lincoln at the Convention in October? Not much. The individual banks, throughout our great land, from sea to shining sea, were supposed to initiate exciting public festivities in honor of 100 Years of Progress Through Service – The Dual Banking System. Believe it or not, I handled a phone call one day from someone who said he'd heard some bankers were "going to hold a public duel" and wasn't that illegal? Was ours a great country or what?

Again, with the aid of JWT [J. Walter Thompson] and excellent support from Joe Fehrenback's Printing Department, we assembled a large Centennial Kit, mailed to all ABA member banks, the press, government, state associations, etc. An elaborate collection of ideas, suggestions, forms, press releases, etc., etc., etc. designed to stimulate individual bank participation in each community.

. . . And then there was the budget. For some reason, thank God, I didn't have to keep the books. I have a faint memory of something like $100,000 being mentioned, which did not include JWT's fees, salaries, travel, etc. I logged a number of miles trying to hold the enthusiasm among ABA's members in check. Did a damned good job if I do say so myself. . .

The 1963 ABA Convention held in Washington at the DAR Hall was where we put the Centennial to sleep. Sandwiched between Gen. Curtis LeMay, Commander of the Strategic Air Command, and Donna Axum, daughter of Hurley Axum, banker from Eldorado, Ark., and the reigning Miss America (real nice girl), the Dual Banking System made its own thunderously successful pre-emptive strike with none other than President Abraham Lincoln. The DAR was never so blessed.

Responding to an electrifying introduction from the podium, which I may even have written or more likely Bob Howard wrote, lights lowered, Honest Abe strode to the stage from the back of the hall to the stirring notes of the Battle Hymn of the Republic. His appearance and brief remarks of gratitude to the bankers for support of his National Currency Act were electrifying and as he retraced his entrance the audience was on its feet delivering an ear shattering standing ovation. If there were any dry eyes in the room, I could never have found them through my own tears. I don't know who that guy was, but he was good. . .

That was it. The rest is a very short history. I didn't get fired. The last day of the Convention, I found an envelope slipped under my door at the Mayflower. I had a new title, Deputy Director, Marketing Division, and a spectacular salary raise to $19,000. . .

I was away from ABA much of the time during the last several months of 1963 and early in 1964, seeking a Presidential appointment to the FDIC's Board of Directors. According to the financial press, at that time I was the clear front-runner and a decision was expected before the end of 1963. Then the tragic assassination of President Kennedy occurred on November 22, 1963, and that event changed many things. There was a new President: Lyndon B. Johnson. I was not nominated for the position I was seeking, and I resumed my full-time schedule with ABA, probably in February or March 1964.

When I was back focusing my full attention on ABA matters, Archie K. Davis, Chairman of the Board of Wachovia Bank and Trust of Winston Salem, N.C., had been elected Vice President of the ABA, a stepping stone for him to become the ABA President in 1965-66. As the new Secretary of the State Bank Division, I would be working with Archie much of the time. He had already delivered his acceptance speech, making it clear that he was going to devote the major portion of his time as President of ABA to improving and strengthening the dual banking system, of which he had been a long-time supporter and admirer. This was a subject about which he was exceptionally knowledgeable, and I had no doubt that he had devoted much of his time as Vice President of ABA to developing his program for his Presidential year.

Dual Banking's Last Great Hurrah? As I described earlier, the ABA's work in the early 1960s was upbeat and celebratory. But it was not at all the story that Archie Davis had in mind for 1965, when he would become ABA President. Dual banking is often described, correctly, as making possible a vigorous and competitive banking system, continually refreshed with a flow of new ideas and new entrants. A quite different but also an accurate expectation was that it could serve as a powerful defense against unduly restrictive government supervision or, even more particularly, as protection against stultifying government regulation. Moreover, and quite differently, it can provide sound banks with important strategic options. It is all of this that makes dual banking so important to the banking industry. And this was what was worrying Archie, who was not yet ready to celebrate. There were important matters to be addressed first. Archie intended to direct the program personally. He took the role that was theoretically assigned to banker Presidents of the ABA, but which was most often handled by the ABA's Executive Vice President (Executive Manager). This observation of mine is not based on any special information. I was just certain that Archie and Charlie Walker would already have worked out the situation, if indeed a question even arose. I was reassured further by Archie's high opinion of Charlie Walker, whom he had singled out for special praise in his opening remarks to the full convention, ending with: "I am convinced that there is now no trade association in America better staffed and better equipped to represent its industry than is your American Bankers Association."

I was delighted by the decision that Archie Davis had made and was looking forward to an interesting several years. Personally, I had planned to establish my own bank-consulting firm, now that the position at the Federal Deposit Insurance Corporation had disappeared. I expected to leave ABA shortly. But I had decided that I could be more helpful to Archie if I remained for his full-term as ABA President, which would run through 1966.

At the ABA's 92nd Annual Convention in Washington, D.C., Archie Davis's Presidential address took the form of a report to the banker audience on his activities during his Presidency. He began by "confessing" his almost complete "preoccupation with the problems affecting our dual banking system," beginning with the bad news first. Relying on several important ABA studies, he told the large banker audience that: "It has become increasingly apparent that all is not well at the state level," and that in too many of our states, bank supervision has not been "fully adequate." Moreover, what may have been even more disturbing to his listeners was his conclusion that the state banking system, "long a primary innovating force," was now tending to lag behind the national bank system in modernizing banking statutes.

Archie then described the way in which he had identified the problems facing the individual states. He had scheduled in advance, and completed, 12 regional meetings of banking leaders from, he said, "every one of the 50 states." All of the meetings were held within the first 10 weeks of his Presidential term. He was able to do this because he did not seek to have large numbers of attendees at each of the 12 meetings. Instead, working primarily with state association officers and key bankers, he had identified before each meeting the persons who were known to have strong opinions, in various ways, about dual banking, as well as a record of expressing views rather than just taking notes. As a result, each of Archie's regional meetings usually had only from 15 to 20 persons. Every one of these meetings was, he said, "completely off the record," and was "remarkable for its candor and objectivity." Also he noted that the regional meetings had confirmed the bad news with which he had opened the sessions at the convention. And just incidentally, knowing Archie, I would have been willing to bet that he counted every person who attended each regional meeting and probably could have confirmed the fact that at least one person had been present from every single state, as he had promised.

Archie announced that a Permanent Steering Committee had been established to guide the program since it would not be possible to complete within a single year (or even several years) the work that had to be done. He identified the members of the new committee, who were the Presidents and Vice Presidents of ABA's prestigious policy committees: the State Bank Division, the National Bank Division and the Trust Division. Archie also included several from the State Association Section and the Chairman of the State Legislation Committee, together with several designated members from those committees. I did not hear in his remarks anything that seemed to require action of some kind by the convention so I assumed that this had already been accomplished and that the first meeting of the Permanent Steering Committee would take place shortly, which in fact it did.

Among the recommendations made at the regional meetings was a strong suggestion that a nationwide workshop was needed on state banking laws. This was arranged by Archie and was held in May 1966. I attended that meeting. Archie reported that it had the "full and enthusiastic support, of the state association managers," which was certainly the case. He noted that delegates were present from 43 states and the District of Columbia, and that the demand for more information was so great that he was now making arrangements to publish the proceedings.

Also growing out of the regional meetings was a strong suggestion that the ABA provide, in addition to its model state banking code, a special manual that would analyze in depth key banking issues of significance for those persons engaged in revising their current state banking statutes. I was placed in charge of this activity, responsible for writing several of the sections and for editing the entire volume. It turned out to be a volume with 17 sections and 386 pages, with provision for additional loose-leaf pages in the manual. The first edition was distributed in 1967 – on target.

I believe that I participated in a few of the regional meetings. Preparation of the special volume that I just described, and my departure from ABA to establish a new business, probably made a perfect attendance record impossible. Unfortunately, I did not keep track of the persons in ABA who were particularly helpful in writing or checking various sections. I can only plead that because many decades had passed, my memory is just not that good, but I do want to express my appreciation to all those from ABA, and there were more than a few, who helped in the preparation of the volume I am discussing here.

I think it is interesting to note how Archie Davis was able to launch the heart of his program – 12 separate regional meetings that together would cover "every state in the Union." He added at the end of his brief Presidential acceptance speech: "To make sure this program is not delayed, we plan to hold the very first meeting right here in Chicago – tomorrow morning." In other words, Archie was telling the audience that work on his program would begin the very next day – the first day of his occupancy of the Presidential office. Ordinarily, the time between the end of an annual convention year (usually in September or October) and the various holidays such as Thanksgiving and Christmas along with the usual end-of-year parties, were not times when very many meetings were scheduled. However, the people Archie wanted to see at the first meeting had been alerted so that it could be held in Chicago. The remaining 11 meetings would be held in other locations over the next several months. The results would then be discussed at a dinner meeting, probably in late December, attended by senior officials from federal banking agencies and hosted by Archie Davis. It was then that Archie would describe the basic reactions to the program.

I believe that this was quite a departure from usual proceedings. I was one of the persons whom Archie singled out at a staff meeting early on the last day of the Chicago convention to round up other senior staff members who would be free to attend a special session at which Archie would lay out his program. It was tradition among ABA staffers to relax on the final convention day unless they were tied up with some last-minute business, which would be the case for only a few staff members. Frankly, I was a little concerned because of the ways in which various persons would ordinarily relax and with the timing of Archie's offer. I breathed a sigh of relief as I watched the staff adjust to the idea of a late, unscheduled session, particularly because if one looked closely enough at a few of the faces in the meeting room it was apparent that some staffers had been celebrating prematurely. Still, all turned out well. The staff seemed quite pleased with the attention given to them by Archie, since it was clearly a program of major importance. Moreover, only Archie was in a position to describe that program accurately.

I left the ABA in 1966 to form Golembe Associates, a banking research and consulting firm headquartered in Washington. The next 23 years of my career were devoted to Golembe Associates, which was acquired in 1989 by BEI, Inc., an Atlanta-based firm specializing in the enhancement of bank earnings.

Chapter Six
An Intervening Episode: My Quest for the FDIC Chairmanship

My unabridged Random House Dictionary tells me that the preferred meaning for "Interlude," (my first choice for this chapter's title) is "an intervening episode," which fits far better. In virtually all of my writing I have taken for myself the position of an interested, knowledgeable (sometimes opinionated) commentator. It has rarely, if ever, been as the principal player. The exception was my decision, some 45 years ago, to seek a Presidential appointment as Chairman of the Federal Deposit Insurance Corporation.

Why Did I Decide to Seek the Nomination? The first reason was that the position I was seeking was not merely an FDIC Directorship. It was clearly a stepping stone to the FDIC Chairmanship in 1963 or early 1964. At that time the FDIC's Board of Directors consisted of three persons, two appointed by the President plus the Comptroller of the Currency. The Comptroller also was a Presidential appointee who served on the FDIC Board in an *ex officio* capacity. Not more than two members of the Board could be from the same political party. The Federal Deposit Insurance Corporation Act provided that the Chairman be one of the two appointed directors, selected by the three members of the Board, not by the President. Given these provisions, plus the fact that the terms of the two appointed directors were six years each, it sometimes created a problem to arrange to have the Board majority from the same party as the President, although this was usually accomplished. However, in this instance rather convincing rumors were afloat that an arrangement had been reached among the White House, members of Congress and other government officials that it would result in the Republican appointee to the FDIC Board becoming its Chairman.

This kind of arrangement was not unprecedented, particularly when a good working relationship existed between the Senate Majority Leader and the Senate Minority Leader, two key lawmakers in the confirmation process. Such decisions, when made, were almost always adhered to, and this was enough for me to decide to proceed. Otherwise, I would not have been interested. Later, I checked the record of the person who had obtained the Republican seat (the seat for which I was contending) and found that, as a Republican, he served as Chairman for five consecutive years of his six-year term. Slightly longer than four years was under a Democrat President and about a year and a half was under a Republican President. The strength of these kinds of arrangements is illustrated by the fact that there had been a dramatic change – the assassination of President Kennedy – between the time of the apparent agreement and the time of the selection of the people to take the various positions. Although the assassination certainly changed a great many things, it did not alter the arrangement that apparently had been made earlier.

The second reason for my decision to seek the FDIC Chairman's position involved the challenge it offered. This, of course, is what virtually every candidate for a Presidential appointment claims, but in this instance I had something different in mind. As I saw it, the FDIC during my time there in the 1950s had been an agency that focused on doing the things it did exceptionally well – bank examinations and dealing with bank failures – with no significant direction from the FDIC's Board of Directors. There was one problem, however. In my nine years with the FDIC, and given the kinds of assignments I had relating to speech writing and occasionally preparing testimony for one of the Directors, it had become clear that FDIC policy had been to avoid taking positions on as many controversial banking issues as possible, even on those where the outcome might be of great importance to the future of the FDIC.

I never understood why top management continued this policy into the 1950s and early 1960s. The only explanation that I could think of was that the FDIC Board had remained rooted in the past, when the paramount objective had been the preservation of the agency itself. The campaign against federal deposit insurance had been exceptionally powerful. Professor John Kenneth Galbraith of Harvard University observed that the American Bankers Association led the fight against the plan "to the last ditch." The ABA even called for President Roosevelt to veto the deposit insurance bill after it had been enacted by Congress, holding it to be "unsound, unscientific, unjust, and dangerous" as well as otherwise unsatisfactory. There was a continuing drumbeat of predictions from many quarters that this latest plan would suffer the same fate (bankruptcy) that had been met by most of its predecessors. In such a setting, the FDIC had been wise to do its job as efficiently and as quietly as possible, using every permissible device to build its reserves, even at times at the expense of depositor recoveries. By the 1960s, the FDIC had demonstrated beyond any question that it was strong and solidly based, but for some reason the Board continued to act as if it were in great danger.

There had been three Chairmen during my time at the FDIC. The first was Maple T. Harl. He succeeded Leo T. Crowley, who had served as Chairman for 11 years, from about the time of the FDIC's creation until 1945. Crowley had been a strong leader, powerfully connected within the Roosevelt Administration. Harl, the Chairman when I arrived, served as such during the remainder of the Truman Administration until the election of General Dwight D. Eisenhower in 1952, after which he continued as a Director. Harl was replaced as Chairman in 1953 by the Republican Director, Henry E. Cook. Cook, in turn, was succeeded in 1957 by Jesse P. Wolcott, who was Chairman during the remainder of the time I was at the FDIC. (I left in 1960.) All three – Harl, Cook and Wolcott – had considerable experience in banking, directly or indirectly.

Harl and Cook had been state superintendents of banking in Colorado and Ohio respectively before being appointed to the FDIC Board. To me, as an historian, it was a delight to work with Jesse Wolcott when he later became Chairman, in part because he was always willing to discuss the origins of the FDIC. As a Congressman from Michigan in 1932-33, Wolcott had played a very active role in the early negotiating sessions, including meetings with President Roosevelt, originally an opponent of deposit insurance. Wolcott remained in Congress, often holding prestigious positions, until President Eisenhower appointed him to the FDIC Board. He ceased being FDIC Chairman when Mr. Kennedy was elected President and was planning to install his own man as Chairman of the FDIC. (Wolcott remained on the FDIC Board as a Director until August 1964.) All three of the gentlemen I mentioned – Harl, Cook and Wolcott – followed the policy of keeping the FDIC uninvolved in almost anything that had to do with banking legislation unless it directly affected the FDIC.

In earlier chapters I have described instances when the FDIC, facing pressure from other agencies, simply retreated. One example was when criticism from one or several agencies apparently led to the 1953 decision by the FDIC Board to order Clark Warburton to cease publishing his outstanding articles dealing with the origins of the Great Depression and the causes of most bank failures during that period. This was not one of the FDIC Board's finest hours. Another example was when the FDIC's strong supporters in the Congress brought forth new legislation in 1950 that would give the agency the power to act in emergencies, particularly if the Federal Reserve refused again to assist in dealing with the problem of massive numbers of bank failures. In that instance, the FDIC failed to counter the Fed's vigorous attempts to water down the language of the FDIC's amendment. As I described in Chapter Two, more than 20 years would pass before a powerful FDIC Chairman, Frank Wille, disregarded the old interpretation and used the power it gave to the FDIC to deal with the nation's first billion-dollar bank failure in 1972. That failure involved Philadelphia's First Pennsylvania Bank. Once Wille broke the logjam, the FDIC used the amendment in a number of other large bank cases, including the failure of the nation's eighth largest commercial bank, Chicago's Continental Illinois, in 1984.

Returning to the situation as it existed in the first several years of the 1960s, the ultraconservative attitude of the FDIC's Board had not escaped the attention of the nation's financial press. Thus, when President Kennedy let it be known that he intended to name Joseph W. Barr, a Treasury official and former Congressman from Indiana as the Democratic appointee to the FDIC Board and when, at about the same time, Jesse Wolcott made known his decision to retire from his Republican seat on the Board, the press greeted this as major news. This was not because Barr's name would be quickly recognized by many outside of Washington or Indiana, and not because I or the other candidates for the Republican seat on the FDIC Board were well-known. Under ordinary circumstances, and assuming that these various changes, in fact, took place, some attention would be given to them by the trade press, and ignored for the most part by the national press. The significant difference in this instance was the importance of what was likely to happen to the FDIC itself.

Richard F. Janssen had a long article in the *Wall Street Journal* early in January 1964 giving his view of what was likely to happen. Understandably, most of the article dealt with Barr's views, since he was accepted as someone certain to be placed on the Board shortly. Janssen was quite specific as to why this was important:

> Unlike some of his predecessors, Mr. Barr suggests that he won't be averse to presenting an FDIC viewpoint to Congressional committees. Frequently, banking observers say, the FDIC has avoided testifying with other agencies on legislation affecting banks, and when pressed to appear, it would try to schedule its witnesses at times when they would draw the least attention.

Janssen also attracted some attention when he wrote:

> The Board can be expected to be more of an innovator and
> to broaden its interest in such things as studying foreign
> operations of banks and speeding up payments to depositors
> after closings of insured banks.

Another well-known reporter on financial matters, Eileen Shanahan of
the *New York Times*, had a somewhat different take than Janssen, although
both covered the situation rather thoroughly. Shanahan's article had appeared
earlier, on October 28, 1963, and made note of the fact that state-chartered
banks were beginning to feel menaced by the expansion policies permitted
for national banks by the Comptroller of the Currency. At that particular
time – from August 1963 to January 1964 – one of the Board positions was
vacant and James J. Saxon, the Comptroller of the Currency, was serving
as Acting Chairman. Jesse Walcott was serving as a Director pending his
retirement. Shanahan observed that state-chartered bankers wanted a strong
voice in Washington and did not think they had one for the moment. With
respect to Barr's views, she stated that:

> Mr. Barr is known to have extensive plans for the
> strengthening and expansion of the insurance corporation.
> In particular, he feels the Corporation needs a major research
> division, which it has never had.

The challenge that I saw in the possibility of serving as Chairman
of the FDIC had nothing at all to do with a need for basic reform in the
organization itself. In fact, the agency's performance record was outstanding.
The senior staff's professionalism and spirit were evidenced throughout the
entire organization albeit, on occasion, tinged with arrogance. But a new
banking and economic environment had begun to emerge, and to ignore
it would be tragic. What the FDIC needed most was to reform its Board of
Directors.

The Fateful Day of November 22, 1963. The decision to declare my
intention to seek an appointment to the FDIC Board of Directors was quite
personal. To be sure, I had talked with a number of close friends about this
possibility, including Clark Warburton, shortly before he retired from the
FDIC, and Edison Cramer, Chief of the FDIC's Research Division. At the
American Bankers Association, the only person with whom I discussed this
initially was Paul Collins, one of ABA's top professionals based in Washington
and a close friend. All three saw no reason why I should hesitate and wished
me good luck.

Sometime in April or May 1963, I discussed my plans with Charlie Walker, the Executive Manager of ABA, and Charles McNeill, the new director of the Washington office of ABA. Neither saw any problem with my proceeding and even suggested that if my campaign interfered too greatly with my regular ABA assignments, they could compensate. Personally, I had the strong impression that both Walker and McNeill thought that I was on a "fool's errand." In any event, they wished me well.

My most important task was to find someone who could run the campaign. The first person I approached, Paul Collins, agreed to accept the challenge. This turned out to be probably the best decision I had made in a long, long time. Although Paul was a friend, that wasn't the important thing. As the Director of Information for ABA's Washington office and the Associate Director of ABA's News Bureau in New York, he had regular contact with the press and, even more important, had become quite familiar with the kinds of information that the press desired or did not desire. Finally, and most important of all, Paul had a well-deserved reputation for accuracy and integrity. It is difficult to convey how important this kind of reputation would be for the campaign we soon launched.

Paul and I started by spending time together, often with a few others not associated with the American Bankers Association, laying out some strategies. The first thing we had to do, in our opinion, was to gather banker support. This was still early in the race, and when we began to do so in early June I don't believe that anyone else had announced an intention to seek this particular position on the FDIC Board. Because of the wide number of contacts I had made at the FDIC, not only in the Division of Research but also because of my work with the General Counsel's office involving speech writing along with preparation of testimony, I had a fairly wide range of contacts. With more than three additional years in the ABA behind me, I had broadened those contacts, particularly with bankers who served on my committee as well as several other ABA committees. Paul began his letters and telephone calls to bankers in June and by the end of August he had well over 20 bankers who had endorsed me, many of them bankers of some prominence. He continued building this number until early October 1963.

This turned out to be one of the most important things we did once competition developed at the end of the summer of 1963. The press, in fact, seemed to delight in informing Paul of different names that surfaced. I can't think of anyone entering the fray later who had identified more than one or two announced supporters. However, one candidate – Kenneth A. (Kay) Randall, a banker from Utah – had enlisted the support of the ranking Republican on the Senate Banking Committee, Sen. Wallace Bennett of Utah. Later, Randall's backers never omitted mentioning that the Senate

Minority Leader, Sen. Everett Dirksen (R-Ill.), also was one of his supporters. Although those were powerful supporters, we were not unduly concerned in the months immediately prior to the assassination of President Kennedy. I had worked in Senator Bennett's office in 1957 and had come to know him quite well. Later, when I decided to seek the position of FDIC Chairman, the Senator assured me that if the White House selected me, he would interpose no objection, a quite important promise. As for Senator Dirksen, we had made our own approach to him, relying on a delegation from the Illinois Bankers Association. In any event, the Minority Leader's reputation for obtaining positions for Republicans was well-known, so at least I met his most basic qualification.

Another strategy that we believed quite important involved making it clear at the outset that I was not "the ABA candidate." This was a potential threat to my campaign in part because there already was an ABA connection at the FDIC. Erle Cocke, Sr., the Chairman of the Executive Committee of the Fulton National Bank of Atlanta, had been elected President of the ABA in 1956. At the completion of his one-year term, Cocke was appointed a Director of the FDIC by President Eisenhower in 1957. Then, after Mr. Kennedy was elected President, Cocke was selected as Chairman of the FDIC Board, with a term running until August 1963. In other words, Cocke was FDIC Chairman at the same time that we were contacting bankers in the summer of 1963 for the privilege of succeeding him.

Many persons felt that the quick movement of the President of the American Bankers Association to the Directorship/Chairmanship of the FDIC had been appropriate, but that didn't mean my ABA connection would be ignored in the campaign. Paul Collins, and other advisors we consulted, suggested that if the point were made by competitors that my campaign was somehow or other being funded or supported by ABA, it would end rather quickly. Fortunately, at that point no one had begun vigorously contesting for the position, thus allowing us enough time to make it clear that the organization with which I was most closely attached because of the time I spent there and because of the variety of things I had done there was the FDIC, not the ABA. There is no question that many in the FDIC were pleased by the idea that someone they knew and someone aware of their interests might possibly be appointed Chairman of the FDIC. Meanwhile, as I had mentioned earlier, the national press was focusing on the need to modernize deposit insurance, as well as the importance of having someone join the Board of Directors who had actually been writing and speaking at conferences about the need for a more active, vigorous deposit insurance system. So in that sense, I could have been viewed by some individuals as the candidate of the FDIC, an impression I did nothing to dispel.

During the fall of 1963, with competition for the Republican seat on the FDIC Board of Directors intensifying, we concluded that several more things should be done before the appointments were announced, which we assumed would be in November or December. The first was to make it clear that I did have a home. I had paid little attention to the rule or custom of applicants for appointment to government positions always to designate a home city or state. A state was often better, particularly if it had a large population and some members of Congress, preferably Senators, who shared the applicant's political persuasion. I decided on New York State because I had been born there and did my undergraduate and graduate work at Columbia College and then Columbia University in New York City. One of the advantages of New York was it had a powerful Republican Senator who was close to the Kennedy Administration and whose support was possible. He was Sen. Jacob Javits. If time permitted, we decided to seek his endorsement.

In addition, a number of the people with whom we had been working, particularly in the House of Representatives, often reminded us that it would be good policy and good politics to obtain an endorsement from Rep. Wright Patman (D-Tex.). Patman was Chairman of the House Banking and Currency Committee and a powerful figure in Congress on banking matters. I had a little trouble deciding whether it would be an advantage to obtain an endorsement from Patman because he was not wildly popular among Republicans in Washington, to put it mildly. Patman was a populist as well as a strong (and knowledgeable) critic of the Federal Reserve Board. However, I found no problem with his bent toward populism and shared some of his criticism of the Federal Reserve, so I agreed to see what I could do.

Another strategy suggestion was not something that any of us thought could be easily obtained. We simply didn't know. It concerned Robert F. Kennedy, the Attorney General and President Kennedy's brother. Robert Kennedy was the President's closest advisor and usually played an important role in advising on appointments to various positions. As it happened, some publicity about the competition for the Republican seat came out at about that time, declaring me the front-runner. That prompted a telephone call from the Attorney General's office, suggesting that I might want to meet with several people from his office to discuss my interest in this appointment. Actually, it sounded more like a demand than an invitation, but nonetheless I accepted. Word came back that a meeting in about two or three days would be useful. We scheduled a meeting at the Willard Hotel coffee shop at 7:00 a.m., which at that time would likely to be deserted. A few comments on these three items may be of some interest.

Our first priority was Senator Javits. Our initial inquiry to his office indicated that he might be willing to endorse my candidacy, but he was tied up with important hearings in New York City, which I believe involved new information about the Mafia. The Senator's staff also pointed out that he had a policy of not endorsing anyone whom he had not met and with whom he had not had some conversation on key banking issues. As it happened, the ABA's 1963 convention was in Washington that fall and I, of course, was there. Since the time was tight, I went to see ABA's Executive Manager Charlie Walker, who was also at the convention in Washington, and asked if he could help. Charlie mentioned that David Rockefeller, then the CEO of what would become Chase Manhattan Bank, was dropping by the convention office very soon and might be of assistance. At that point, Rockefeller walked in, and Charlie immediately briefed him on the situation and asked if he would mind making a telephone call to Senator Javits setting up an appointment for me. Rockefeller said he was quite willing. He made the call, had a nice conversation with Javits and hung up the phone. He said that Javits had agreed to interview me very soon, and I agreed that I would leave the convention and be in New York at the time selected.

I was not at all surprised at Rockefeller's willingness to set up the appointment since Paul Collins had already been in touch with him on several occasions. Rockefeller had followed up with conversations and favorable letters on my candidacy to Senator Bennett and the Secretary of the Treasury, Douglas Dillon.

The interview went quite well. It turned out that Senator Javits was involved in an investigation of some Mafia matter where mobster informant Joe Valachi had turned on the rest of them, and the testimony had been receiving a great deal of publicity. The Senator could only duck out of the hearing room for a short time because he had an important role to play – both as a key Senator and as the former District Attorney of New York. Our conversation was brief, but pleasant. It resulted in his endorsement.

Obtaining an endorsement from Congressman Wright Patman proved to be not all that difficult. I knew and liked several members of his staff. The Congressman was a long-time caustic critic of the Federal Reserve, while my views on monetary policy had me classified as an "independent." Because of the work we had done earlier, no one regarded me as "the ABA candidate." That was quite fortunate because the ABA was not one of Patman's favorite organizations. On the other hand, my previous association with the FDIC was an asset in dealing with Patman. At the time, the FDIC was much better known and more powerful than in later years; it was still thought of as "the agency that ended bank failures." Interestingly, once Mr. Patman gave me his support, which he did in a letter to President Kennedy, I began to realize the importance of that endorsement.

Our overture to the Attorney General was a different kind of challenge. Indeed, it posed something of a problem, starting with the interview I had with several members of the Department of Justice staff at the Willard Hotel. The problem arose over the Attorney General's long-term investigation of Jimmy Hoffa and recent reports of questionable financial dealings. To my surprise, the major interest of the several sharp, but rather young, DOJ attorneys centered on how much help I could be in connection with the Hoffa investigation. It was clear that they assumed I was aware of the investigation, which I was, and that I recognized its importance, which I did.

What they really wanted was access to bank examination reports, which were close to sacred and regarded as strictly confidential. As I recall, I said that I could not permit a "fishing expedition" through the examination reports, but would be willing to check with the FDIC's attorneys to see how much latitude I had, if any. I added that if an actual crime or something tangible was at the center of their investigations, I could conceive of circumstances in which it probably would be possible to make information available from the examination reports. But again, I suggested that I would have to work carefully with the FDIC attorneys, who were much more knowledgeable about this subject than I. The DOJ attorneys didn't seem happy with my responses but, on the other hand, they didn't seem to be terribly offended.

Soon thereafter I received a call from one of my supporters at the House of Representatives who had just received word that the Attorney General's office would pose no objection to my appointment. In fact, my friend began the conversation over the telephone by saying: "Good morning, Mr. Chairman!" He would prove to be quite wrong. President Kennedy was assassinated a few weeks later, which made it possible that everything could change.

My guess is that millions of Americans alive then can recall today precisely where they were and what they were doing at the moment that they learned of President Kennedy's death. My personal reactions probably were widely shared: bitter anger and deep sorrow. This comes from a person who had not voted for Mr. Kennedy in 1960 and likely would not vote for him in 1964. Nonetheless, he truly represented a class act among U.S. Presidents. I felt that his death was a great loss.

On the fateful day, November 22, 1963, I was in New York City to participate in a fairly large ABA conference at the Biltmore Hotel. I had just left the ABA's headquarters building in Murray Hill, a short eight blocks from the Biltmore, with the radio's announcement ringing in my ears: "the President has been shot but there is no further news." As I walked briskly up Madison Avenue toward the Biltmore, suddenly – almost as if it had been choreographed in Hollywood – someone seemed to be emerging from every building on each side of the street unfolding a flag and hanging it at half-mast. I finished my walk in a daze, but I will never forget that array of U.S. flags stretching as far as the eye could see. I have not the slightest recollection of what I did or said when I reached the hotel. The President was dead.

The Johnson Administration's Impact on Our Campaign. Of course, the world eventually came back into focus, probably in about two or three days. In my case the immediate question was the status of the FDIC appointment. Something that had seemed over and done with, except for the formality of a routine Senate confirmation hearing, now appeared uncertain. On the surface, all should have been well. I had touched all the proper bases, obtained the essential endorsements and made the useful contacts. The press made occasional mention of a group of seven or eight persons – I think that one of these was to be a member of the Federal Reserve Board – who had expected to be in their various positions by late 1963 or early 1964. I was sometimes included in this group. Probably all of us were trying to decide what, if anything, had happened as a result of the assassination.

As of the date of President Kennedy's tragic trip to Dallas, our campaign had reached its peak strength and seemed likely to be successful. Banker reaction had been remarkably favorable. In June we began contacting bankers I had known or worked with and by the end of August we had about 20 bankers – the CEOs or senior officers from large and small banks – pledged to support my candidacy. Among the larger banks represented were the Bank of America (Jesse Tapp, Chairman of the Board), Mellon National Bank in Pittsburgh (John Mayer, President) and Chase Manhattan Bank (David Rockefeller, President). Among the smaller institutions, Thomas Cooper of Jefferson State Bank in Iowa; Otto Kotouc, President of the Home State Bank in Humbolt, Neb.; and Willis Alexander, CEO of the Trenton Trust Company in Trenton Mo., were typical. Many of the bankers we contacted had in turn contacted other bankers and, perhaps even more important, federal officials, usually the Secretary of the Treasury. At least two bankers wrote directly to President Kennedy.

A group of Republican Senators promised their support. Included in this group were Sen. Jacob Javits from New York (a member of the Senate Banking Committee) as well as Sen. Thurston Morton of Kentucky (Chairman of the Republican Senatorial Campaign Committee), Sen. Hugh Scott of Pennsylvania and Sen. Frank Carlson of Kansas. To me, one of the surprising people to support my campaign, in a particularly strong letter to President Kennedy, was House Banking Committee Chairman Wright Patman of Texas. There was only one problem with my campaign at that juncture: it was the campaign devised for an Administration about to undergo significant change.

To be sure, the depth of that change did not seem immediately apparent. For example, some thought that President Kennedy's brother, Robert Kennedy, might continue in his position as Attorney General and, therefore, be a force in the Johnson Cabinet. There was even some excited talk that Robert Kennedy might be a candidate for Vice President in the forthcoming national election in 1964, as President Johnson's running mate. This was by no means something that President Johnson wanted to see happen, and apparently the same conclusion had been reached by Robert Kennedy, who soon resigned his position as Attorney General and went to New York to campaign – successfully it turned out – for the available Senate seat there.

None of these and other plans involving a relationship between Robert Kennedy and Lyndon Johnson were realistic. It was no secret that the two gentlemen disliked each other intensely. This ill will deepened during the Kennedy Presidency and continued after the assassination. As one commentator put it: "No affection contaminated the relationship between the Vice President and the Attorney General . . . it was a pure case of mutual dislike."

The single most important political change resulting from the assassination was that Lyndon Johnson had suddenly become the major player in fashioning and implementing the Administration's legislative program. To be sure, the program for 1964 had been worked out by President Kennedy and his principal advisors, including the Vice President, and there was no important change in that regard. But the key players responsible for carrying out the program, including the Presidential nomination process, would likely be different, a matter important to, among many others, Paul Collins and me.

For the first several years of his Vice Presidency, Lyndon Johnson usually had been given a subsidiary role in dealing with Congress. At least among his friends, Mr. Johnson railed against the Kennedy Administration's waste of his experience and expertise, particularly in the case of the Senate. Suddenly he had both: the power of the Presidency and the ability to ride herd on those not accustomed to daily management by the President. As for the program itself, President Kennedy and the Vice President had been in agreement that the most important legislative goal, albeit the goal most difficult to attain, was to see a strong Civil Rights Act become law before the 1964 elections. Most politicians and pundits considered the prospect for success as grim, or even totally unrealistic, primarily because of the strength of the Southern block of Senators. Then suddenly, Lyndon Johnson assumed command.

One of Mr. Johnson's biographers, Robert Dallek, wrote that: "Johnson knew what he wanted to do with civil rights. From the moment he assumed the Presidency, he saw a compelling need to drive Kennedy's bill through the Congress with no major compromises that would weaken the law." This bill would force an end to the system of racial separation at public facilities across the South. Johnson was determined to accomplish this through new legislation even though he also was aware of the fact that it would be extremely difficult. As a matter of fact, Mr. Johnson needed passage of such a bill much more than President Kennedy had. In 1963, Mr. Johnson was not regarded as a reliable advocate of a civil rights statute of this magnitude because he had been part of the Southern group that traditionally refused to let any such legislation through the Senate.

The fact was that, personally, Johnson was a true believer in the merits of strong effective civil rights legislation. To be sure, there was no split between him and his Southern Senate friends, but he made it clear to them from the outset that he was intent on getting some new legislation. Moreover, he intended to make certain that it would not be watered down – like previous civil rights legislation. He also believed that his future as the President depended on his firmness on civil rights. According to Dallek, Mr. Johnson told one correspondent: "I knew that if I didn't get out in front on this issue [the liberals] would get to me." Speaking to Doris Kearns he said: "I had to produce a civil rights bill that was even stronger than the one they'd have gotten if Kennedy had lived. Without this, I'd be dead before I could even begin."

A major problem for the President was, despite his popularity among Southern Democrats, they would never vote with him on the civil rights issue. There was only one possibility open to him, and that was to persuade Senator Dirksen, the Senate Minority Leader, to come out for the bill and, even more importantly, to persuade a number of Republican Senators to vote for cloture if the measure was filibustered by the Southern Democrats. As Johnson put it very frankly to Sen. Hubert H. Humphrey (D-Minn.), who was in charge of shepherding the bill through the Senate:

> Now you know that this bill can't pass unless we get Ev Dirksen. You and I are going to get him. You make up your mind now that you've got to spend time with Ev Dirksen. You've got to let him have a piece of the action. He's got to look good all the time.

It was evident that President Johnson would need the votes and help that Senator Dirksen could provide. President Johnson had assumed the same role that he had when he was Senate Majority Leader. Accordingly, he could be expected to go for assistance to those persons on whom he had depended in the past. Everett Dirksen, the Republican leader in the Senate, was one such person. He and Mr. Johnson had developed a solid working relationship over the years, particularly when Mr. Johnson had been Majority Leader. And although it might not have received much attention at the time, almost immediately after Mr. Johnson became President he deputized Jack Valenti to be his personal representative to Republican leaders in the House and, most importantly, to Senator Dirksen.

Against this background, Paul Collins came up with the idea of trying to finesse my nomination by a quick and early move before the White House and Congress got bogged down with civil rights in 1964. Paul had some friends at the *Washington Post*, as did I. They had been following the contest for the Republican spot on the FDIC Board and were quite enthusiastic about my candidacy. We persuaded them that an editorial calling upon the President to appoint me to the FDIC Board would be helpful. It appeared on Sunday, December 29, 1963. It contained a strong and forceful endorsement of me. It made no mention of my competition. Rather, it implied that the appointment had been intended to occur several months ago, but had been delayed by the assassination. In tone, the editorial appeared to suggest that this was merely a piece of unfinished business that Mr. Johnson should complete.

This notion appeared to be confirmed by something that happened, I believe, in early January. Joe Barr had received his appointment as Chairman on January 22, 1964, although it is quite possible that he was physically in place prior to that date. From August 4, 1963 to January 22, 1964, James J. Saxon, the Comptroller of the Currency, had been the Acting Chairman of the FDIC. Quite possibly it may have been during this time that Joe telephoned me to ask for some help on several important FDIC staff appointments about which he had no real information. My guess is that he did not want to ask his only other fellow Board member, Jim Saxon. In any event, I did go over to the FDIC and made several suggestions about individuals with whose abilities I was quite familiar. I believe that my suggestions were accepted. Joe and I talked briefly. The only thing I remember was that he hoped that my appointment would come through fairly soon so that we could work together as had been anticipated. However, this would be the last time I heard anything about this, and I mention it only because it confirms my impression that although the assassination had occurred on November 22, at least in the following five or six weeks my candidacy was apparently still alive and well. I also had the impression that Joe himself was anxious to move on, although he did not say anything about this. As it turned out, he served as FDIC Chairman for about a year and a half, and later served a brief term as Secretary of the Treasury.

As a matter of fact, the appointment of Joe Barr as FDIC Chairman and my appointment as Director had long been treated by the press as something that would happen at the same time. For example, the October 21, 1963 issue of *Washington Financial Reports*, published before the assassination, contained a notation that "President Kennedy had already announced that he would nominate Joseph W. Barr . . . to replace Erle Cocke, Sr., who retired in August." And then it went on in a heavily underlined sentence, to say that there were strong indications the Republican minority nomination will be sent to Congress at the same time that the White House formally submits Mr. Barr's name. Although it did not say explicitly that the two appointments would go together, we were clearly regarded as a pair. Of course, that is what was implied in the *Washington Post* editorial as well. In fact, the editorial went a bit further: "[Golembe's] candidacy is widely supported in Congress and the banking industry, and is most enthusiastically backed by Joseph W. Barr, whose nomination as Chairman of the FDIC will soon be sent up to Capitol Hill . . ." Referring to me, the editorial concluded with the statement: "We hope that the President will not pass over an opportunity to appoint a strong man to a critical post in the FDIC."

Even though a tandem announcement of the Barr and Golembe nominations did not materialize, the *Washington Post* editorial did give me a boost and worried my major competitor in terms of possibly influencing Senate Dirksen, who had a noted ability to come up with all kinds of positions for Republican appointees. Several years after the publication of the editorial, I happened to run into Kay Randall's principal assistant, John Lee. He told me that the editorial had severely panicked Kay's supporters, who were banking on Dirksen's support, and that he and Kay had a few rough days. This has often made me wonder if we should have waged a more aggressive campaign after the *Washington Post* editorial appeared, using our supporters to approach Dirksen and the Johnson White House, but we realized time was running short.

Robert Dallek's fine biography of President Johnson does not disclose precisely how or when President Johnson persuaded Senator Dirksen to move more Republican votes to his side of the table on the Civil Rights Act of 1964. But by pure chance I gained some insight from an article in the *New York Times* on June 24, 2005. The article was an op-ed piece headlined "The Best of Enemies" written by former White House staffer Jack Valenti. In it, he was reminiscing about the old days when he had been charged by President Johnson with staying in close touch with the Senate Minority Leader. What surprised and fascinated me was that Valenti used the 41-year-old Civil Rights Act as the centerpiece for his article. Valenti wrote about a past in which collegiality, not enmity, characterized relationships in the

Congress, particularly in the Senate. In this article, Valenti did not give dates or other specifics, but it was clear that in very broad terms, he was talking about the Civil Rights Act of 1964, one of the most famous pieces of civil rights legislation in the United States.

Describing a "typical encounter," Valenti said Senator Dirksen might call him, asking if he could see the President sometime that evening. Valenti would say "of course," and suggest dropping by around 6:00 p.m. The President and Dirksen would then have a fairly long conversation on recent events. Then at one point, the President might say something like: "Ev, I need three Republican votes on my civil rights bill, and you can get them." Dirksen, in turn, would pull out his list of openings to which Republicans could be appointed, and there would be some brief, general discussion. There was no way you could tell that the President and Senator Dirksen, who left shortly after, had reached a serious agreement. As Valenti put it, there would be no summary of what they had said. "Their relationship built on something that is sorely missing today: trust. Both of them knew that plenty of quarrels would be played out on the Senate floor . . . but they also knew once a commitment had been made, it would be kept." Significantly, Valenti went on to observe that: "If they had disagreed, then they would have kept on talking."

There was a Southern filibuster on the civil rights bill. It had lasted for 75 days, after which a cloture vote was called. The President and Senator Humphrey got more than the 67 votes needed; the actual vote to end the debate was 71-29, and the President signed the Civil Rights Act into law on July 2, 1964 on a national telecast.

The fate of my campaign for the FDIC Chairmanship was sealed several months before that. I learned of the exact date fairly recently when I stumbled across a transcript of a recorded telephone call on February 5, 1964 from President Johnson to Sen. Wallace Bennett, the Utah Republican who was a leading figure on the Senate Banking Committee. This phone call demonstrated how deeply Mr. Johnson was now involved in the nomination process and that the Attorney General was no longer a factor.

The President made it clear that this was a Republican appointment and he would go along with the recommendation of Bennett and Dirksen, the Senate Minority Leader. The President read from a memo he had received from Treasury Secretary Douglas Dillon. "Both [Golembe and Kay Randall] should make good members [of the FDIC Board]," the Dillon memo said. "Golembe has considerably broader experience in banking and has the support of vocal elements in the American Bankers Association. Randall is not well-known in banking circles, therefore does not seem to have any support in this area, but this should not be counted against him."

"[It is our understanding that while Senator] Bennett is strongly in favor of Randall, his second choice, if he had one, would be Golembe, who served . . . as his special assistant." the Dillon memo continued. Senator Dirksen made an early commitment on this to Senator Bennett, but has been under considerable pressure from the banking fraternity indicating [it is not opposed to Golembe]." The Treasury Secretary's memo concluded by saying that the President "would not go wrong by choosing either candidate."

The President pressed Bennett on his preference for Randall. "Oh, that's right," Bennett responded. "He's a hometown boy, you know. He's a home-state boy . . . But they're both good men."

Mr. Johnson reflected briefly on the geographic background of the two candidates, noting that New York, my home state for the purpose of this nomination, is a lot bigger, but that he liked Utah and the people there. "They are pretty conscientious, earnest people, and they put their country ahead of their party and anything else. I talked to [Mormon] President McKay about this boy [Randall] the other day. [The Mormon leadership] thought he'd make a fine fellow, so I'm going to go ahead and follow your recommendation."

The President also made it clear that "I'm going to do it [nominate Randall] on your account and Everett's account because I think if the positions were reversed and you were the ranking man [on the Senate Banking Committee] and I was the Democratic [Minority] Leader, that you'd certainly give consideration to [my wishes]."

According to the FDIC's records, Kenneth A. Randall became a Director of the FDIC on March 10, 1964. He filled the Republican seat left by the retiring Jessie B. Wolcott. About one year later the arrangement long-anticipated took place, with Randall elected FDIC Chairman on April 21, 1965 (my birthday, incidentally). He served a full term as Chairman in both a Democrat and then a Republican administration, stepping down in early 1970. When Randall came to Washington, I arranged to meet him and congratulate him. I found him to be an interesting and pleasant person, and we had several social meetings over the next four or five years.

My wife and I "celebrated" the end of the FDIC campaign with a huge (for us) party to which we invited everyone who played any part in our campaign and their spouses. An astonishingly large number attended, and I wish it possible to list them all here. At the party there were the inevitable discussions of what might have been, but the major subject was the future.

Not long after the FDIC appointment struggle ended, I received an appointment to be Secretary of the ABA's State Bank Division. The Division staff moved to Washington, but there was no change in my responsibilities in the Washington office. But neither was there a conflict since the State Bank

Division was preparing to launch a major nationwide campaign to enhance and modernize state banking laws and procedures. While this had always been a matter of importance, the success achieved by the Comptroller of the Currency in 1962 and 1963 for national banks had given a dramatic new intensity to the State Bank Division's responsibilities.

Chapter Seven
The Saxon Revolution and Its Aftermath

Rarely does a bank regulator have the ability – and the opportunity – to change the course of U.S. banking and financial history. James J. Saxon, the Comptroller of the Currency from 1961 until 1966, was such a person. As administrator of the national banking system more than 40 years ago, he set out to lift the burden of stifling government regulation from national banks and thus indirectly from all banks. He did not seek to do this in cooperation with the other federal banking agencies. In fact, he believed that the administrators of the other two most powerful agencies – the Federal Reserve and the Federal Deposit Insurance Corporation – were part of the problem and not part of the solution. His campaign, therefore, was a lonely one in Washington, but was greeted with much enthusiasm by many bankers and economists located outside of the Washington Beltway (and more than just a scattered few inside). Jim Saxon did not enjoy complete success in this campaign, although he did chalk up some notable victories. By the time he had completed his five-year term, he had set in motion changes in the nation's banking and financial system that are still working themselves out.

There have been other great Comptrollers of the Currency, quite possibly some more able than Jim Saxon, but not very many. But there were few who faced so daunting a problem and who also possessed the necessary amount of independence that Jim Saxon had – or took. For in response to a variety of economic pressures – some structural and some competitive – banking in the late 1950s was faced with the problem of adjusting to a seemingly intractable regulatory framework of outdated laws and regulations – a framework designed specifically to hold banking back.

The Agency. The federal agency that Jim Saxon administered was, and is, unique and powerful. Probably its name is not as familiar to the average person because the title is so strange. It is known officially as the Office of the Comptroller of the Currency (the OCC, for short). My dictionary defines the word "comptroller" simply as "controller," with the notation that long ago there was some initial confusion over the proper spelling of that word. In any event, the OCC has virtually nothing to do with the volume of currency or, more broadly, the nations circulating medium. But it did at one time as I described in the Introduction to this volume.

The creation of a national currency came during the Civil War and for obvious reasons was something very much desired by President Lincoln and the Secretary of the Treasury, Salmon P. Chase. The President and the Secretary were probably the two individuals most responsible for the legislation in 1863-65 that created a national currency. Specifically, the National Bank Act and various amendments thereto put the federal government in the business of issuing charters for national banks, institutions that had not previously existed, and gave the currency privilege solely to these new banks. Their banknotes were secured by U.S. Treasury bonds so that the nation had, finally, a uniform currency in appearance and one that was absolutely safe.

I also mentioned earlier that Congress was not able to rid itself of state banking even though denying state banks the currency privilege was expected either to prompt them to go out of business or become national banks. But state-chartered banks focused instead on deposit banking, which was becoming increasingly important, and within a fairly short time once again outnumbered national banks, although state banks were generally of very small size. To be sure, Congress had never intended state banks to survive, but it was too late politically to do much about it. Ironically, a century later, the American Bankers Association devoted the whole of its 1963 annual convention to celebrating the 100th anniversary of the "Dual Banking System." The Dual Banking System originally meant two separate systems of banking – one consisting of state-chartered institutions subject to examination and supervision by state agencies and another consisting of federally chartered institutions (national banks) subject to supervision by the Comptroller of the Currency.

The unique position of the OCC was apparent even in its early history. "Independent" federal agencies were not common at that time, but instead were generally incorporated in one fashion or another into the structures of the cabinet agencies. The OCC was made a "Bureau" of the Treasury Department, thus indicating that it was to function subject to the general direction of the Secretary of the Treasury. In today's world, it would have been structured as an independent agency like the FDIC and the Federal Reserve. But even as part of the Treasury, the OCC was a most unusual "Bureau," as Congress made quite clear in the basic legislation. For example, the annual salary of the Comptroller was set at a handsome figure for the time. There also was some early talk of locating the Bureau outside of Washington and making the term of the Comptroller 10 years, neither of which happened. The Comptroller's term of office was finally established at five years, and the agency remained headquartered in Washington. However, appointment to the five-year term was by the President of the United States, and not by the Secretary of the Treasury, and required the advice and consent of the Senate.

Rather clearly, Congress wanted the new agency to have considerable independence. Thus, the Comptroller was not burdened by the existence of a board of which he or she had to be a part. Such an arrangement – beloved by bureaucrats – often means, particularly in crisis periods, that essential decisions are made late or not at all. So instead, the OCC was treated as a cabinet agency, with a single individual in charge. Of course, the Comptroller was required to report to the Congress annually, but the law provided that these reports must come directly from the OCC and not through the Secretary of the Treasury.

To put no finer point on it, the Comptroller was made responsible for administering the federal government's own banking system, and this official has had that responsibility from the day the office was created. The unique position of the OCC becomes clear when the powers of the three federal banking agencies are compared. The Comptroller of the Currency is concerned with a complete banking system while the FDIC and the Federal Reserve have their own clear and quite separate set of responsibilities, in addition to having been given limited bank regulatory responsibilities, particularly those involving bank examinations.

What this means is that the Comptroller charters national banks, or admits operating banks to membership in the national bank system, and closes national banks when circumstances require it. Thus, the Comptroller's objectives must be the maintenance of a safe, competitive, vibrant banking system, with no conflicts of interest because of any outside responsibilities, such as those conflicts faced by the Fed and the FDIC. Specifically, the FDIC and the Federal Reserve cannot charter banks and in exercising their additional regulatory and examination responsibilities over state-chartered banks, they must be careful to deal with the inherent conflicts of interest in these arrangements. For example, the FDIC's clear interest in protecting its deposit insurance fund can be permitted to be so extreme as to prevent every possible bank failure. Banks are, of course, expected to make some loans that are risky while taking steps to protect against excess losses.

The Federal Reserve, meantime, has a variety of potential conflicts of interest with which it must deal. One of particular concern encountered in recent years has been the temptation by the Fed to use its regulatory powers to "persuade" banks it regulates to follow a course of action that it believes to be in the public interest, but that may not be at all in the interest of safe or sound banking, or in the interest of depositors or owners of the particular bank.

This is not to say that the Federal Reserve and the FDIC are incapable of balancing their competing interests because of the structure in which they are involved. Nor does it mean that the Comptroller can always achieve precisely the right balance even though he is dealing with a single system. However, there have been documented instances where these conflicts have not been handled successfully. In fact, in the case of the Federal Reserve's problem, the large majority of advanced banking systems in the world now draw a rather clear line between monetary policy (a central bank responsibility) and hands-on regulation (a regulatory agency responsibility, especially in terms of bank examinations). Some nations, such as the United Kingdom, provide for cooperation between the two agencies, subject to a clear delineation of the responsibilities of each and the various situations that may be encountered. Our Federal Reserve Board is one of the few holdouts, presumably on the ground that supervision and regulation are indeed central bank responsibilities.

It may be of interest that in the last study by a Presidential commission (the Hunt Commission in 1970-71) there were only two important recommendations made with respect to the distribution of supervisory and regulatory powers among the federal banking agencies. First, the Federal Reserve should no longer be involved in bank supervision or regulation, particularly bank examinations. Second, the FDIC should no longer be involved in insuring bank deposits, but should have full responsibility for examinations and supervision of all state-chartered banks, including the state-member banks now overseen by the Federal Reserve. These recommendations were at the time thought to quite likely be adopted, but were wiped out in 1973-74 when public policy debates were trumped by the Watergate scandal.

The Person. I don't know how much advance planning Jim Saxon did before beginning his term as Comptroller of the Currency, but my guess is not very much. He had 25 years of extensive experience in many facets of commercial banking. Moreover, he was familiar with the banking industry's political interests and various important divisions within the banking industry.

He began his career as a securities statistician in the Office of the Comptroller in 1937 and, much later, was to spend some time as Assistant General Counsel in the Washington office of the American Bankers Association. He also served as a Special Assistant to Secretary of the Treasury John W. Snyder in the Truman Administration, and later became an attorney at the First National Bank of Chicago. President Kennedy nominated him as the Comptroller of the Currency in November 1961.

Sharp-eyed readers may have noted that the appointment was announced almost one full year after the election of Mr. Kennedy. This may have been because the Kennedy staff – possibly Robert F. Kennedy, the President's brother – was not very experienced with Presidential appointments at that time. The problem in this instance was that the term of the incumbent Comptroller still had about four years to run. As I recall, the problem (a cause of hilarity among newspaper reporters) was settled with some slight-of-hand by the Attorney General. As the new occupant of that position, Robert Kennedy ruled that anyone serving a fixed term who had resigned before the end of that term at the request of the President was deemed to have completed his or her term and, therefore, was not required to spend a specified period of time outside of the banking industry before joining the management team at any bank. But all of this took a little time so that I assume that Jim Saxon had a fairly long opportunity to lay out his plans for the next five years.

I was not a close personal friend of Jim Saxon. I only knew Jim on a professional basis, although hardly just casually. As the new Secretary of ABA's State Bank Division, it was expected that my staff and I would keep close tabs on what the new Comptroller was doing. A bit later in this chapter I will describe the ABA's reaction to the Comptroller's campaign, which may surprise some readers.

Personally, I came to have a strong admiration for Jim's objective and, I think, at least an understanding of his tactics. He was a rough campaigner and might have profited by seeking more cooperation from the other federal banking agencies. However, at the same time I had strong doubts that he would have, in fact, received much cooperation, or at least until considerable time had passed. I suspect that Jim thought he did not have the luxury of time, if he were to serve only a single five-year term as Comptroller. In any event, my own conclusion was that someone with Jim's background and personality was probably necessary to break through the regulatory wall that was suffocating the banking industry in order that, as Jim himself had put it: "proper scope is allowed for the exercise of individual initiative and innovation."

While Saxon was in office, I did have a few personal experiences that involved him.

In 1961, before Jim had taken office, but was known to be coming aboard soon, I had traveled to the ABA's Washington office to arrange for my own transfer from New York. When I arrived, I found the Washington staff busily making arrangements to call off a function scheduled to honor the new Comptroller, who at one time worked in that office himself. However, it turned out that the ABA had gotten a little ahead of itself and had just found out that Jim was not going to appear, having decided that it was inappropriate for a federal bank regulator to be honored at a reception hosted by a lobbying organization even before he was in office. I was honestly impressed. It appeared that the easy familiarity and coziness between regulators and the institutions they regulated might be coming to an end, which I thought was indeed proper.

There was no question that Jim Saxon was a man passionately caught up in the causes he espoused, so much so that those who opposed him were viewed in less than a kindly light. That happened to me once. I was working in the Washington office of the ABA on a Saturday along with two secretaries who were handling my dictation. About noon the three of us headed for the Washington Hotel where we were going to lunch (the ABA headquarters was then just north of Pennsylvania Avenue, very near the Treasury building and the Washington Hotel). The two secretaries with me had known Jim when he was on the ABA staff and admired him tremendously. At that particular time there had been a controversy between the ABA and the Comptroller's Office on some matter or other, and it was understood (correctly) that I had something to do with writing the ABA's response. Just as we reached the side entrance of the Treasury, out popped Jim Saxon, alone. We ABAers greeted Jim with a chorus of "hellos," but he looked at us in silence with a cold stare of non-recognition. At lunch, one of the secretaries burst into tears.

The only real confrontation between Jim Saxon and me occurred at about the same time. In March 1962, President Kennedy had created an interagency Committee on Financial Institutions. "The general task of the committee is to consider what changes, if any, in Government policy toward private financial institutions could contribute to economic stability, growth and efficiencies," Mr. Kennedy said. The committee was headed by Walter W. Heller, Chairman of the President's Council of Economic Advisers. It consisted of the Secretary of the Treasury, the Attorney General, the Secretary of Agriculture, the Director of the Bureau of the Budget, the Chairman of the Federal Reserve Board, the Chairman of the Federal Home Loan Bank Board, the Administrator of the Housing and Home Finance Agency, the Comptroller of the Currency and the Chairman of the FDIC. With the President's top economist as its chairman, the committee was nicknamed the Heller Committee. In most instances, a senior official, say from the Federal Reserve Board or the Treasury, would represent the principal member at the committee's meetings. This was not true of all of the members, including Erle Cocke, Sr., the Chairman of the Federal Deposit Insurance Corporation.

Cocke called me after the committee's organizational meeting and asked if I could arrange with the ABA to spend some time during the next year working with him on this prestigious panel, attending the meetings with him and on occasion acting as his representative when he could not be present. Cocke assured me that he had cleared this arrangement with the powers that be on the committee, and I never gave it a second thought, even though I was at that time no longer employed by the FDIC, but by the American Bankers Association. I cleared Cocke's request with Charlie Walker, ABA's Executive Manager, and began using a small office at the FDIC that Cocke had arranged.

I also began attending the committee's meetings once or twice with the FDIC Chairman and once or twice by myself. At about the fourth or fifth meeting, Saxon still had not made his first appearance, but on this occasion he sent a senior OCC official as his representative. The Attorney General also had sent a Justice Department official as his representative. With Cocke and me both present, we were stunned when Saxon's representative and the Attorney General's representative proceeded to ask for permission to introduce a new subject for discussion – namely, the inappropriateness of having an official of a banking trade association engaged in the deliberations of a high-level committee on federal banking policy. The complaint had been initiated by Jim Saxon, who was not present. As the representative of the Attorney General recited the various statutes and regulations that would be violated by my presence, I began to worry. I had regarded the committee as essentially a discussion group, but it was clear that the Attorney General's representative did not share that view. He said Cocke and I had been violating the law.

Cocke was quite irritated by this charge and insisted that my position as his representative had been cleared at the initial meeting of the committee, which I had not attended. The problem with Cocke's protestation was that the secretary of the committee pointed out that the minutes of the first meeting made no mention of any discussion of my assignment or Cocke's intentions. Things were looking bleak until two members of the committee suddenly spoke up and said that, in fact, they did recall Cocke raising the issue at the organizational meeting. The dispute was resolved by, first, amending the secretary's minutes to document Cocke's intentions, but, second, asking me to relinquish my seat on the committee and leave the room. I was delighted. Although Saxon was primarily irritated at Cocke, it wasn't a pleasant experience for me. However, I never mentioned the episode to Jim. The Heller Committee on Financial Institutions issued its report to the President in April 1963. The report covered the scope and structure of reserve requirements, interest rate regulation, portfolio regulation, federal charters for financial institutions, insurance of deposits and (credit union) shares, structural changes and competition among financial institutions, conflicts of interest (among officers, directors and employees of financial institutions with other business interests), and supervision and examination of financial institutions. Jim Saxon was, of course, a signatory to that report.

My personal experience included a glimpse at the thoughtful side of Jim Saxon's nature. In 1967, after he was out of office but still in Washington and not very long after I had organized Golembe Associates, I received a phone call from him. This was at a time when the going was rocky and clients were few. Jim asked if I could visit him at his office in the next day or two. I wondered what he had in mind, and it turned out to be nothing more than a sincere offer of assistance if I needed any secretarial support or any other kind of help in getting a new office established. There were no strings attached, and I was quite grateful. But I told him that I thought I could pull this thing off myself, which, as it happened, I did.

In Washington, one often learns more about a person from the stories that circulate about him or her than from any other source. Between 1961 and 1966, Washington abounded with stories about Jim Saxon, of which I estimate 70 percent were grossly exaggerated. All that was important was that they were told, and also often believed. They presented a picture of a smart, dynamic individual, intent for whatever personal and professional reasons, on "shaking the cage" – that is, seeing to it, almost single handedly, that commercial banking was brought out from under the suffering cocoon of regulation into the competitive world of the 20th century. It is often said that it was the bankers whom Jim Saxon wanted to shake up. Not so– at least not importantly so. It was clear that Saxon had the support of the great majority of the bankers, even many small bankers, and as far as I can determine, almost 100 percent of economists. For the most part, it was his fellow regulators that the Comptroller found to be unresponsive and antagonistic toward his ideas. Needless to say, they did not appreciate the attention he showered upon them.

Few persons in my opinion could so quickly raise the hackles of the Washington establishment. There was even an effort by Congress to "investigate" Saxon's various policies, particularly those relating to chartering banks and acting on mergers. The investigation went nowhere. Although his tenure as Comptroller was marked with continuous strife, Saxon enjoyed the fight.

Banking Industry's Mood. Commercial bankers were a restive, concerned group in 1960. Many, especially those with the larger institutions, were beginning to chafe at the burden of regulation, most of which had been imposed in the late 1920s and early 1930s. The reason commercial banks were singled out for onerous regulation was in part because they were deemed to be "special" in the sense that they had an exclusive authority, at least at that time, to offer demand deposit facilities. So powerful was this demand deposit authority believed to be that policymakers sought to maintain a banking structure that consisted of thousands and thousands of individual commercial banks. This was thought to be a way of avoiding any concentration of economic power in the hands of a small number of banks.

One element of heavy regulation on commercial banks in 1960 was the use of geographic limits on where banks might do business. For example, in 1960 no bank could have offices located beyond its state line, and within each state the extent to which it might have offices was determined by the state law. In that regard, the states fell generally into three categories – 1) those that permitted banks located in the state to operate branches at locations throughout the state, 2) those that permitted banks located in their state to branch less than statewide (say, in their home city, county or a designated district), and 3) those that prohibited branching altogether. The latter were called "unit banking states." Several major states, including Illinois, were in the unit banking category. So Chicago banks, however huge, had no real authority to expand their business in the state. Meanwhile, non-bank financial businesses generally could do business across state lines, even nationwide, but not commercial banks. For all practical purposes, the Bank Holding Company Act of 1956 prohibited interstate mergers or acquisitions. So the only evidence of interstate banking after 1956 was in "grandfathered" situations, such as two large bank holding companies headquartered in Minnesota that had acquired banks in North Dakota, South Dakota and Montana years earlier.

A second element of heavy regulation of commercial banks that was particularly burdensome involved bank powers. In 1960, a commercial bank could make loans and accept deposits – not much more outside of conducting a trust business. A bank couldn't sell insurance as agent except in small towns. It couldn't offer mutual funds, which were about to go big-time in the financial market place. It couldn't operate a securities brokerage business. It could conduct investment banking only to the extent of general obligations – that is, bonds backed by the taxing authority of the issuer, be that the federal government, a state or a municipality. And so on and so forth. In short, a commercial bank's product line was extremely limited.

Of course, these kinds of restrictions cut both ways, in the sense that non-bank financial firms were prohibited from doing a banking business. But the competitive playing field was tilted in favor of non-bank financial firms because they had little difficulty conducting a financial business that was not quite "banking." [Finally in the late 1970s, the credit unions invented a "negotiable order of withdrawal" – the so-called NOW account, which was in effect an interest-bearing demand deposit. At the time, there was a prohibition against paying interest on a commercial bank demand deposit. Congress immediately recognized the competitive implications and voted NOW account authority for all depository institutions, including commercial banks.]

The third and perhaps strangest element of heavy regulation on commercial banks in 1960 was interest rate control on time and savings deposits. As administered by the Federal Reserve under its Regulation Q, interest rate ceilings were established on all time and savings deposits offered by commercial banks, savings banks and savings and loan associations. This deposit interest regulation was motivated originally by the idea that payment of excessive interest had been a cause of many bank failures, which turned out to be a fable. The extra burden on commercial banks was that savings and loan associations were allowed to pay one-quarter of one percent more on the same time or savings deposit as a commercial bank could – the so-called S&L differential. In fact, in California and Hawaii, S&Ls were allowed to pay an additional one-quarter of one percent more. This led to California S&Ls advertising elsewhere in the country soliciting time and savings deposits at higher interest rates than local institutions could pay. I never saw any Hawaii ads, but there might have been some.

Such was the banking structure environment Saxon faced when he became Comptroller of the Currency in 1961. The prospect of accomplishing anything really useful must have been grim. To be sure, the future of the U.S. economy seemed bright. The public clearly desired an expanding group of services, many of them quite new, and made possible by the new technological advances, such as the computer. But the problem for the Comptroller was that he was saddled with a complex set of rules and regulations dating back to the depression years of the 1930s and even further.

The Saxon Legacy. My impression is that Jim Saxon came to his new task as Comptroller quite focused on his strong belief that regulatory controls must be fashioned "so that proper scope is allowed for the exercise of individual initiative and innovation," a view that was obviously not true at that time in his opinion. That there would be no uncertainty as to his position, he announced in an early OCC Annual Report that the agency was examining each of the rules and regulations to which national banks were subject in order to determine their usefulness in promoting bank safety. And then:

> Whenever a restrictive control did not meet this test, we have endeavored to broaden the discretionary powers of the national banks . . . The purpose throughout has been to secure for the nation the fullest benefit of the capabilities, the initiative and the enterprise of bankers in the national effort to promote the maximum growth and development of the economy.

I also am sure that Jim had a pretty clear fix on the kind of anticompetitive laws or rules that should be dealt with early on, as well as where the most opposition would come from once his work got underway. Moreover, shortly after taking office he queried all national banks on their opinions for needed changes in law or policy, and then appointed a commission of 24 bankers and lawyers to review all of the responses (not all of which he agreed with) and to make recommendations by the end of 1962. The commission met that deadline.

One of the commission's recommendations was that the title of the agency should henceforth be the Administrator of National Banks. Another was that the agency should be made independent of the Treasury. As things happened, no final action was taken on the various recommendations of that commission, except that it appears that the title Administrator of National Banks began to be used in conjunction with the title Comptroller of the Currency – and still is to this day. Interestingly, the same commission recommended the establishment of a new agency – the Administrator of State Banks – into which would be placed all of the supervisory and regulatory powers of the FDIC and the Federal Reserve, essentially taking the central bank out of bank regulation and the FDIC out of its deposit insurance responsibilities, which would be transferred to a new agency set up to oversee all government guarantee programs.

Reform of the kind envisioned by the Comptroller was facilitated or would be facilitated by the fact that his office had the ability to expand the powers of national banks, although not without challenge in the event that it was alleged that he had exceeded the authority inherent in his statute. New legislation was not a good way of proceeding because of the time required and the likely opposition of the other banking agencies, including many of the state agencies. However, Saxon did have a major legislative triumph in his first year in office when Congress transferred to the Comptroller from the Federal Reserve the regulatory power over the trust business done by national banks.

The importance of the Saxon program is not found in a mere tabulation of wins and losses. What made his work significant was an understanding of the reaction of the banking industry and of the banking regulators. Together, these reactions had a significant influence on the changing banking industry.

The bank reaction was not uniform. National banks, and large banks generally, were quite favorable, though not completely. For example, David Rockefeller, the CEO of Chase Manhattan Bank, was not a fan of Saxon in at least one respect. In 1963, he was an outspoken critic of Saxon's action allowing First National City Bank (now Citibank) to open 26 branches in the New York City suburbs while Chase, a state-chartered bank, had been authorized only eight branches by the New York State Department of Banking. But banks that liked Saxon were impressed with the early and continuing evidence that the Comptroller was coming forth with a veritable flood of new rulings. He allowed national bank trust departments to offer a full range of fiduciary services. He authorized national banks to underwrite revenue bonds and to offer (mutual fund-like) commingled managing agency accounts. He permitted national banks to engage in direct financing of personal property leasing. He authorized national banks to accept savings deposits from profit-making corporations. He ruled that national banks in towns of more than 5,000 could operate insurance agencies even though the National Bank Act simply said national banks in towns of 5,000 and less may do so. Well, he seemed to reason, the law didn't say national banks in the larger towns could not operate insurance agencies. There were a host of other rulings as well. Not surprisingly, some of these rulings were challenged and in some instances the Comptroller had to pull back (for example, on underwriting revenue bonds, offering commingled accounts and operating insurance agencies in larger towns), while others became significant new banking powers (such as national bank lease financing of personal property). But even when the Comptroller was challenged and ultimately lost, he was applauded by many bankers for taking direct action, especially in cases where a restraint on national banks was downright silly. Such was the case with underwriting revenue bonds. The Glass-Steagall Act of 1933 permitted banks to continue underwriting the general obligations of states and municipalities. But Glass-Steagall contained no mention of revenue bonds, primarily because they were of little consequence in 1933. General obligations were backed by the taxing authority of the issuer. Revenue bonds depended on the proceeds from turnpike tolls and the like. By the early 1960s, when Saxon made his ruling, revenue bonds were in widespread use. Even though it could be argued that the absence of express language in Glass-Steagall authorizing bank underwriting of revenue bonds was little more than an oversight, the courts disagreed.

When it came to banker reactions to the Saxon regime, the voting was, in effect, done by choice of charter, and in that regard Jim Saxon had clearly struck oil. In the five years from 1962 through 1966, the number of state-chartered banks that converted to national charters totaled 115, but only 41 national banks converted to state charters during the same timeframe. Not surprisingly, it was the larger state banks that moved into the national system, while it was the smaller national banks that went in the other direction, so that there was a net transfer of $17 billion of commercial bank assets from the state to the national system, a significant amount 45 years ago.

In terms of the relationship between the Comptroller's office and the Federal Reserve, it might be noted that all state-chartered banks converting to national charter were, by doing so, opting to be members of the more expensive system in terms of examination and regulatory costs. This was because the Federal Reserve charged essentially nothing for its examinations and related activities, while each national bank paid to the OCC the full cost of its examination and regulatory activities. To be sure, state-chartered banks paid an examination fee to the state bank regulator that had chartered its bank, but the amount was usually quite modest. In effect, a state bank transferring to the national system was giving up a substantial subsidy in joining the national system.

In other words, banks that converted to national charter were saying that the value of the national charter was superior to that of the state charter. For the Federal Reserve's cherished "state member bank" system, the consequences were catastrophic. Data for the full decade 1956-66, heavily influenced by the 1962-66 period, show that there were 37 states in which the number of state-member banks had declined, often drastically. In several states, the number had fallen by more than 50 percent – for example, from 33 to 14 in California, from 7 to 2 in Oregon, from 91 to 37 in Pennsylvania, and from 16 to 13 in Connecticut. Impressive declines had occurred in other states as well. Consider that there were 153 state bank members of the Federal Reserve in Michigan in December 1956, but 10 years later only 114. In New Jersey over the same period, the decline was from 59 to 44, and in New York from 130 to 83. Banks were moving heavily into the Saxon camp, and in many instances voting to walk away from the regulatory reach of the Federal Reserve. The trend didn't tail off until Saxon left office. Among Saxon's claims to fame is the fact that bankers probably gave him the greatest vote of confidence of any bank regulator in history.

If Saxon's liberalizing rulings did not infuriate his fellow regulators, then his chartering and merger policies certainly did. He simply rejected the idea that bank chartering policy should be governed to any significant extent by an effort to protect operating banks against new competition. He solved the matter by issuing new charters. From 1962 through 1965, 514 new national banks (and 498 new state banks) began operations. This may be compared with only 99 new national banks and 341 new state banks organized during the four previous years (1958-61).

The Saxon philosophy on bank mergers, largely continued by his successors as Comptroller, was simply that the competitive realities of the marketplace should dictate his decisions, rather than the esoteric theories or arcane rules of academicians or attorneys. By and large, these decisions of the OCC have fared exceedingly well over the years.

In my view, the important legacy of Jim Saxon is that he set in motion a chain of events that altered the face of the commercial banking industry through the rest of the 20th century. He was far from perfect, not always wise and certainly not always successful, particularly in the short run. But he saw what had to be done with a clarity and breadth of vision that is rare in a government administrator. One would like to believe that imbedded in the philosophy of every regulatory official, whether in banking or any other industry, there will be found Saxon's belief that a major criterion for regulation is, as he put it, to "fashion the controls so that proper scope is allowed for the exercise of individual initiative and innovation." Perhaps even more importantly, one wishes that regulators who subscribe to such a belief would fit their actions to their words.

Chapter Eight
Reflections

Fast forward to 2002. That was the year I ceased publication of The Golembe Reports, which I began writing in 1967, the year after Jim Saxon left office as Comptroller the Currency and I left the American Bankers Association to start my own banking and economics consulting firm, Golembe Associates, Inc. I wrote The Golembe Reports continuously for 35 years and produced about 10 of them a year on average, usually running 10 single-spaced, typewritten pages long, but sometimes longer.

My last Golembe Report was published April 8, 2002. Like this chapter, it was titled "Reflections" and focused on many of the issues I wrote about and consulted about over the previous 35 years as well as some of the people I met along the way.

The Last 35 Years. I mentioned in that last Golembe Report that during the previous several decades, the number and importance of changes in the business of banking and in the banking industry itself, attributable to changing public policies affecting banking, have been truly remarkable. Yet for those who lived through that period, it is also a remarkable fact that, with only one significant exception, nothing that happened would have been surprising or unexpected. This takes a bit of explaining.

All change in banking does not spring from the same source. The single most important driver of change is always the free market. It works ceaselessly to undermine restrictions on what it is possible to do, helped in no small way by the computer and information revolutions of recent years. The market, for example, has no respect for the idea that financial firms engaged in basically the same kind of business – moving funds from where they are in surplus to where they are in demand – should be distinguished by the way they go about this. I refer, of course, to banks, investment banks and insurance companies.

Economic history textbooks often find it convenient to mark changes by the significant statutes enacted by the U.S. Congress. Thus, territorial restrictions on banks were removed by the Riegle-Neal Act in 1994. Banking was "modernized" in 1999 by the Gramm-Leach-Bliley Act and so forth. The fact is that these and most other such legislation simply confirmed that which the market had already largely done (and would continue to do even in the absence of legislation), leaving Congress the task of cleaning up the rubble left behind and, admittedly, making final changes a bit smoother.

Of course, change comes on occasion for other reasons, such as the increasing interest in protecting consumers from real or fancied abuses by banks, the first manifestation of which was the Truth in Lending Act of 1968. This was followed by a long string of new laws, usually including in their titles such words as "Truth" or "Fair," but also the powerful Community Reinvestment Act, a 1977 law seeking to ensure that banks serve the entire communities in which they do business. Most of these measures were directed largely or entirely at commercial banks and savings associations.

Change comes often from still another source. I refer to the never-ending search by regulators for their "Holy Grail" – a simple formula or ratio that will encompass all that is needed to eliminate messy, hands-on supervision by tough, experienced examiners. In the 1960s and 1970s, it was thought that interest rate ceilings were the ideal answer, but in 1980 the market forced Congress to terminate the ceilings in the Depository Institutions Deregulation and Monetary Control Act. Later the focus of regulators turned to capital ratios, which they received power to regulate in 1983. As has been demonstrated early in the first decade of the 21st century, capital ratios by themselves are not a sure-fire guarantee of a bank's health and well-being.

Finally, there is the change often resulting from what the financial press likes to call "turf warfare," but is really something much more important. For example, the significance of bank holding companies as operating, regulated entities was essentially a U.S. phenomenon. It reflected a conscious effort by the central bank (the Federal Reserve) to replace the Treasury as the dominant banking regulator in the United States. That battle has been going on for decades and tends to continue in one form or another.

Still, the industry is accustomed to the kinds of changes produced by market forces, by aggressive regulators and by consumer advocates, with results that may be good or bad. Earlier I mentioned that there had been one significant exception to my claim that most public policy changes in banking could be anticipated once one knew their source. It was the completely unexpected and, therefore, shocking to most people, announcement by the U.S. Supreme Court in 1963 that banking was subject to those portions of the antitrust laws involving mergers, particularly Section 7 of the Clayton

Act. Apparently the assumption had always been that the United States had so many banks that, whatever the number of mergers, there could not possibly be a tendency toward monopoly, and that bank mergers were, accordingly, something to be encouraged or, at least, ignored by the courts. In the Philadelphia case in 1963, the Supreme Court took a quite different and quite unexpected view. *United States v. Philadelphia National Bank*, 374 U.S. 321 (1963).

To say that there was consternation among lawyers and others working with banks would be an understatement. Indeed, our modest array of consulting economists at Golembe Associates suddenly found, to our great delight, that even the most prestigious law firms sought us out – and, of course, other groups of economists as well – on the question of assessing and evaluating the impact of the Supreme Court's opinion. It was not very long before law schools began providing new courses dealing with the implications of the Supreme Court's decision. The year 1966 was a great time to go into the business of economic consulting for banks!

Possible Future Events. In that last Golembe Report in 2002, I mentioned a couple of unresolved public policy issues that may have to be addressed over the years immediately ahead. Not surprisingly they are issues that have resurfaced in the wake of the financial crisis of the early 21st century.

The most significant unresolved public policy issue, I said then, is a need for deciding upon the proper role for the central bank in the U.S. financial regulatory system. My view has always been that there should be a clear separation between the supervision and regulation of banking organizations by bank chartering agencies on the one hand and the central bank on the other. Many persons agree with my view, but probably there are as many who disagree.

The rationale for those who believe that the central bank should hold the dominant position with respect to supervision and regulation of financial institutions – the "umbrella regulator" is the usual term – has traditionally been that the Federal Reserve has broad, macro-economic responsibilities, whereas the other agencies concerned with supervision and regulation of banks and savings associations have much narrower responsibilities, essentially focusing on safety and soundness. Moreover, as Federal Reserve Chairman Alan Greenspan told the Senate Banking Committee in 1994, in time of crisis the central bank can make good use of the "clout" (his word) that comes with having regulatory power.

The counter-argument has traditionally been that adding the supervision and regulation of banks and other financial activities to the already awesome power of the central bank can lead to serious problems of imbalance at the highest levels of government. Moreover, it means facing, and finding solutions for, significant conflicts of interest. It is a serious mistake to believe that the chartering agencies, such as the Comptroller of the Currency or state agencies chartering banks, are concerned only with safety and soundness. They cannot be and should not be. In the case of the Comptroller, for example, the responsibility of that office is the proper administration of the federal government's own banking system (comprised of national banks) and carries with it, in addition to safety and soundness considerations, the need for the Comptroller to assure that the national banking system is healthy, vigorous, competitive, profitable, innovative and capable of serving in the best possible manner the banking needs of its customers.

The question facing the United States in the early 21st century is one that most other countries have already faced in recent years. Virtually all have resolved it by insisting on the separation of central banking from supervision and regulation. On the other hand, it is recognized that both the central bank and the regulatory agencies must share responsibility for financial stability and must work closely to achieve that objective. The United States has lagged behind other nations in dealing with this most important issue. Yet it did face it quite clearly at an earlier time in our history – in 1832 in the so-called bank war, when President Andrew Jackson ended the "war" by vetoing the re-chartering of the Second Bank of the United States, our first central bank. One result was the disappearance of central banking in the United States until 1913, some 77 years after the Second Bank's charter expired.

The determination of the proper role of the central bank in the nation's financial regulatory system is of vital importance. It should not be decided behind the scenes, or caught up in and included in a much different legislative matter, or depend on the power or prestige of any particular individual. The solution is far too important to be reached before receiving the full and open attention of the entire financial community and the Congress.

Another major unresolved issue that I said needed early attention in 2002 is the matter of the Federal Deposit Insurance Corporation and the role that it will play in the future. What concerned me was that the reforms then under consideration were not of very much significance. For the most part, they involved operating changes and housekeeping details, some of which may be quite useful. But nothing of major significance was under consideration, with the exception of a possible change in the level of deposit insurance coverage.

There are, of course, a number of important FDIC-related issues that must be addressed at some point, I said then. For example, is the federal government's deposit guarantee commitment better handled by another, possibly new, agency? The Hunt Commission in 1971 made such a proposal, recommending that the FDIC's supervisory role (and title) be changed to make it the Administrator of State Banks, responsible for supervising and regulating all state-chartered institutions at the federal level, including those now supervised and regulated by the Federal Reserve, while moving the collection and distribution of insurance funds to a separate agency. The basic rationale for this, and similar proposals that continue to surface on occasion, was not new. It was simply that it may be inappropriate (i.e., a conflict of interest) to have in the same agency supervision and regulation authority in addition to responsibility for meeting the obligation of the federal government to see that there are sufficient funds available to cover government's insurance commitment to depositors. This was the specific reason given by the Hunt Commission for suggesting the division of responsibilities.

Another tough task, I said then, was identification of the specific mission or missions of the FDIC. Is the protection, and even the enhancement of community banking, one such mission? This has never been a stated position of the FDIC, at least openly. However, the protection of small community banks was clearly uppermost in the minds of most Congressmen favoring deposit insurance legislation in 1933. Moreover, there is not the slightest question that but for the vigorous support of the thousands of community banks, there would have been no deposit insurance legislation enacted in 1933. But this doesn't mean, necessarily, that this is a proper mission for the FDIC going forward. I was simply suggesting that at some point one must face up to this. Instead, people continue to dance about the issue, with such things as indexing insurance coverage. In the final analysis, whether coverage should be considerably higher or lower depends very much on defining the mission of the FDIC.

People I Knew or Knew Of. When reflecting on spending more than a half-century in Washington, all of it in one form or another dealing with some aspect of banking, I said in that final 2002 Golembe Report that my most vivid memories were not of great events, or of the rise or fall of institutions, or the enactment of historic legislation. Rather, they were simply about people I have known, or have known of, who in one way or another have left a lasting impression, and often had much to do with my thinking.

One such person was Dwight D. Eisenhower, the 34th President of the United States. He was a person whom I did not know. In fact, I doubt that I ever met him (although I served under him in the infantry in 1943-45). Mr. Eisenhower was one of those unfortunate Presidents who, in my view, presided over a nation that was prosperous and at peace during his eight years (from 1953 to 1961). For the media and the historians, this meant that he attracted little or no interest. Fortunately, as time passes, it has become increasingly apparent that the reason for that peaceful and prosperous time was due in large part to the way in which the Office of the President was administered by Mr. Eisenhower.

One of the knocks against President Eisenhower was that offered by Theodore H. White, a noted authority and historian who dealt with Presidents and Presidential elections during the period from the 1950s until about the mid-1970s. White was, in many ways, an admirer of Mr. Eisenhower but his judgment of his ability as President was as follows:

> [Eisenhower's] view of the Presidency was simple: Congress passed the laws, the Supreme Court judged the laws, the President did his best to execute the laws. [Apart from one noted exception involving Senator McCarthy] he never gave any show of understanding the manipulative political power and responsibility of the Presidency.

There is a personal angle to my recollections about Dwight D. Eisenhower. In 1957, when I was a financial economist in the office of Sen. Wallace F. Bennett, a conservative Republican from Utah who served on the Senate Finance Committee, my principal job was to work with the Senator on forthcoming hearings concerning the state of the economy and Federal Reserve policies. This was the first year of President Eisenhower's second term, and I had paid relatively little attention to what else was going on in our office. Probably most important at the time was the Republican-originated, strongly supported civil rights bill – the first such piece of legislation to come before the Congress since Reconstruction. The bill was narrowly drawn, dealing only with voting rights, and would not justify much mention in histories except for the fact that it was the first such legislation to come before the Congress in 82 years.

One morning I arrived at the office very early and found the Senator's top aide there, looking very strange. I asked if anything was wrong and he told me that he had just come from breakfast with the President. It turned out that he had received a telephone call the previous evening asking him to join the President for breakfast. When he arrived he found several aides of other Republican Senators also present. The President was not there, but one of the attendants suggested that the aides proceed to eat, which they did, after which the President walked in. Mr. Eisenhower did not sit down and join them, I was told, but instead made a very short announcement. His remarks, as described to me, were: the Republican Party regards the civil rights bill as a key piece of legislation; the Republican Senators for whom the assembled aides work were reported to be unenthusiastic or even opposed to the measure; it was the responsibility of each of the aides to see to it that his or her Senator did, in fact, vote for the bill; if a favorable vote was not received, the personal future of those present at the breakfast was likely to be grim. Then the President walked out. The civil rights bill passed, and I do not recall if indeed the President was able to get those particular votes, but I assume that he did and I have always assumed, although I never asked, that Senator Bennett had gone along. Bennett was a remarkably loyal Republican and thought very highly of the President. Ironically, *The New Yorker* of April 1, 2002 contained an article about Lyndon Johnson, attributing passage of this historic piece of civil rights legislation primarily to his efforts while he was in his first term as Senate Majority Leader (after the Republicans narrowly lost control of the Senate). There was no mention at all of any interest or activity by President Eisenhower, which probably is exactly what the President intended.

Another person who I deeply admired was Ben DuBois, Mr. Independent Banker. He was one of the most interesting gentlemen I have ever had the opportunity to meet. He hailed from Sauk Centre, Minnesota and was one of the founders of the organization now known as the Independent Community Bankers of America.

I have a special reason for remembering Ben DuBois. In the 1950s, although I had been at the FDIC for some time, no one official from outside the Corporation had ever invited me to lunch. Ben spent a great deal of time at the FDIC, meeting and chatting with people, which was not particularly difficult because at the time the entire agency occupied just three and a half floors of the National Press Building. I knew him by sight and had been introduced to him. One day the door to my office opened and there was a booming voice: "Hey young fella, how about joining me for lunch?" By lunch he meant at the old Willard Hotel, which then, at least to my eyes, was even grander than the lavish restored hotel. The lunch was fascinating, and I am not certain that what I remember is completely accurate. For example, I think Ben said that he had come to Sauk Centre in a covered wagon and that one of his close childhood friends was Sinclair Lewis, whose best seller, Main Street, was set in Sauk Centre. But I believed him, as well as his other tales about Minnesota in the old days. He also pressed on me clippings of various articles that he thought would be of interest. It was clear that I was talking to a true "populist," in the sense that railroad tycoons, large landowners and large feed mill operators were not his favorite people.

When discussing the 1933 deposit insurance legislation with Ben, I mentioned that large banks were unhappy about the fact that assessments were based on total deposits and not on insured deposits. Ben snorted, saying that large banks had been compensated for this by Congress prohibiting in the same legislation the payment of interest on demand deposits. Such interest had previously gone largely to small country banks holding their reserves and other deposits in large city banks. As Ben saw it, it was the small banks that, in fact, had underwritten deposit insurance coverage. Much later I dug into this matter and was convinced that he was correct – that the two actions were connected. My report on it has since been accepted and often cited. (See Vol. 1975-10, "Interest on Demand Deposits," December 19, 1975)

I got to know Ben better over the next several years. On a trip to Minnesota when consulting with the Minnesota Bankers Association, he invited me to come up to Sauk Centre and possibly get a better understanding of how a small bank operates. On a Friday afternoon I spent most of the time in the bank, where Ben sat in his "office," which consisted of a desk and chair right at the entrance so that he could say hello and goodbye personally to every person who walked in or out of the bank. Occasionally I looked down the street at the competing bank – I think an affiliate of Northwest Bancorporation, one of the largest bank holding companies in the state or country that later acquired Wells Fargo – and did not notice the same level of activity as in Ben's bank. Later that night, after dinner, he and I were looking out of one of the picture windows in the living room when I said to him "Ben, I don't understand why you are so opposed to holding company banking. I didn't see anything much going on in the other bank; you seemed to be doing most of the business." His response was interesting: "Carter, that doesn't make a bit of difference. They're big," meaning the holding company and not its small affiliate in Sauk Centre.

There were a number of other people I encountered directly or indirectly during my career that I will not forget. Many of them were associated with the FDIC. During its earliest years and until 1945, the FDIC was managed by an outstanding individual, Leo Crowley. After World War II, times were generally favorable, bank failures were few and the FDIC was managed, with only a few clear exceptions, by an unremarkable set of chairmen, though in fairness it must be conceded that few were required to face very difficult times. However, two chairmen that I think deserve special mention were those who were in office when extremely difficult situations arose: Bill Isaac, when many large savings banks faced failure in the early 1980s because of inflation and later, when the eighth largest bank in the United States – Continental Illinois – failed in 1984. Then Bill Seidman presided over the FDIC's massive problems of hundreds of bank failures clustered in the late 1980s and early 1990s.

Late in their service, neither Isaac nor Seidman was a favorite of the administration in power. In fact, Isaac's term had expired and the Reagan Administration had refused to reappoint him, but it could not find a successor and, as a result, he served a rather long period after his term had ended.

Bill Seidman, on the other hand, faced a more awkward problem. His term had not expired, but the first Bush Administration made it clear that it did not want him to remain in office. That administration sought his voluntary retirement. Fortunately for the FDIC and the nation, Seidman fought off this attempt successfully and completed his full term, leaving his office in 1991.

Among other things, Bill Seidman was noted for his ability to survive in Washington. What sticks in my mind about him is the note that he sent to me when he was in the hospital. It was during the time that the Bush Administration was attempting to force him out. As I recall, he had an accident while riding his horse. I dropped him a brief note, saying how much I regretted hearing about his accident and wishing him speedy recovery. I am sure many others did the same. An answer came back immediately from the hospital, which was also a very short note thanking me for my good wishes. But written below the typed portion of the letter, in very large letters, apparently in crayon, were the words "I'm not going anywhere." I rather suspect that Seidman added the same message to a great many of his other responses to get-well letters he received, and that this helped end any thought that somehow or other, because of the accident, he would be leaving office.

While I am on the subject of federal officials, some others deserve special mention. Back when Paul Volcker was Chairman of the Federal Reserve Board, I was invited by Preston Martin, the Fed Vice Chairman, to speak informally at a Federal Reserve retreat in Maryland. In attendance were the members of the Federal Reserve Board, key staff members and the Presidents of the Federal Reserve Banks. After dinner, the first question to me came from the President of one of the Reserve Banks. He had obviously prepared himself and had a long list of what he viewed as mistaken statements by me about the Federal Reserve. This was at a time when I was writing frequently about my view that the central bank should not be engaged in hands-on supervision of banking organizations. My questioner's list of disagreements was so long it struck me that it would take the entire evening to deal with all of them. I, therefore, decided to use a ploy attributed to H.L. Mencken. Mencken was said to have answered every letter disagreeing with his views, of which there were many, with the same response: "Dear Sir or Madam: You may be right." The ploy worked, received a friendly laugh, and we cut to a more specific subject.

I still have not forgotten, however, a question from Chairman Volcker during the discussion that followed. As best I recall, it went something like this: "Carter, as a bank historian, deep in your heart aren't you unhappy about the fact that commercial banks make loans on real estate?" This was a tough one, given the conditions he had set forth and I am not certain just what I answered – probably a smart aleck remark. I think I invoked the name of Walter Bagehot, author of *Lombard Street*, a famous 19th century book on the money market. I probably said something like: "Well, I guess Bagehot would not have approved, but times are different and I want to think about it." What it suggested to me was that Volcker, whom I have always regarded, and still regard, as one of the finest Federal Reserve Board Chairmen who ever served, was not only a clever questioner, but also a fundamentalist at heart.

Another remarkable federal official, one who warranted an entire chapter in this book, was James J. Saxon. Saxon was the Comptroller of the Currency for five years ending in November 1966. There is no question that he was responsible, almost single handedly, for bringing bank regulation into the 20th century, a modernization effort that dwarfs in importance those of earlier or recent years.

Then there were many people who contributed more to my education than they will ever know. One of those was Clark Warburton, one of the nation's outstanding economists and for many years the senior economist for the FDIC. Like Saxon, he was an individual who deserved an entire chapter in this book.

The Barnett Connection. As I look back, it strikes me that nothing can quite compare to having been a part, however minor, of a banking organization that under strong leadership and with a little good fortune, and the wind at its back, manages to separate itself from the pack and move upward to become the leader of its chosen locale, whether county, state, nation or internationally. I had the good fortune to be part of one of these occurrences. Which is to say that for about a quarter century, from the 1970s until the mid-1990s, I was involved in one fashion or another in the emergence of Barnett Banks of Florida as it became the dominant banking institution in Florida, and seemed headed for much more.

Barnett was, at the outset, a thoroughly decentralized organization. Its holding company had a large number of banks – all located in Florida. These numbered about 30, plus a number of non-banking organizations. Barnett had only two real leaders during the most important formative years stretching over almost two decades, Guy Botts and Charles Rice. But the thing I remember most vividly, and the person about whom I think often was one of the Barnett Bank presidents on Florida's west coast whose name I can't recall. My largely self-imposed practice, first as a consultant and then as a director of the holding company, was to check continually with the various bank presidents in order to determine how the system was running, whether there were any serious problems and, most importantly, how it might be improved, and then giving my observations to Barnett's Management

Committee. When Barnett was growing most rapidly and employee morale was sky high, I can't think of an individual anywhere in the company who was not convinced that it would conquer not only Florida but eventually the rest of the nation.

The Barnett banker I mentioned earlier was located in a county that had a number of competing banks, the single most important of which was an affiliate of another holding company – a bank whose parent had decided to convert into a branch. This left Barnett's bank the only sizable bank in the area that could milk its near-independent status in competition with, now, a mere branch. When I visited the bank that year I asked the banker what his plans were for dealing with the old competitor, now a branch of a bank headquartered some distance away. The Barnett banker looked at me quietly for a moment or two before responding: "My plan is rape, pillage and plunder." I figured that there was little more to talk about and, sure enough, as I watched the reports over the next year or two, he was correct.

In reflecting on a career that spanned over five decades, I am reminded that banking is a huge, powerful, ever-changing industry with a fascinating present and indefinable future – more so in the early 21st century as the lines between commercial banks, savings banks, investments banks and insurance companies continue to blur or even disappear. Although banking is certainly an ancient business, it is still evolving, and as that unfolds one can only hope that policymakers will shape the regulatory environment for banking and financial services in ways that will best serve the economy and the public interest.

One final thought. A founding partner of one of Washington's most prestigious law firms, Arnold & Porter, is credited with a saying that seems to apply to a memoir like this. It was Paul Porter who was reputed to have said: "As I become older, many of the things I remember most vividly never really occurred." I hope that isn't the case here, but one can never be quite sure.

Notes

Introduction: The U.S. Banking System – And How It Got that Way

1. John Kenneth Galbraith, *Money*. Houghton Mifflin Company, Boston, Mass. (1975), p. 192.
2. Carl Felsenfeld, *Banking Regulation in the United States*. Juris Publishing Inc., Huntington, N.Y. (2002), p.3.
3. Howard H. Hackley, "Our Baffling Banking System," *Virginia Law Review*, Pts. 1&2. (1966), pp. 507, 775.
4. Benjamin J. Klebaner, *Commercial Banking in the United States: A History*. Dryden Press, Hinsdale, Ill. (1974), p. 2. This history was revised, enlarged and updated in 1990, Twain Publishers, Boston.
5. Fritz Redlich, *The Molding of American Banking, Views and Ideas*. Johnson Reprint Corporation, New York and London, Volume One (1968), pp. 6-7.
6. Bray Hammond, *Banks and Politics in America*. Princeton University Press, Princeton, N.J. (1991 and 2001).
7. Ron Chernow, *Alexander Hamilton*. Penguin Press, New York, N.Y. (2004).
8. David Herbert Donald, *Lincoln*. Simon and Schuster, New York, N.Y. (1995).

Chapter 1: The Beginning of My Journey

1. Theodore H. White, *In Search of History: A Personal Adventure*. Harper & Row, New York, N.Y. (1978), p. 404.
2. David S. Holland, *When Regulation Was Too Successful – The Sixth Decade of Deposit Insurance*. Praeger Publishers, Westport, Conn., and London (1998), p. 120.
3. *New York State Assembly Journal* (1839), p. 439.
4. *Congressional Record*, Vol. 77, 73rd Cong., p. 4033.
5. *Congressional Record*, Vol. 77, Pt. 5, 73rd Cong., first sess., p. 4429.

6. *Cong. Rec.* 5897 (1933) (id, at 5886).

Chapter 2: The Attempt to Create An Effective "Lender of Last Resort"

1. Allan H. Meltzer, *A History of the Federal Reserve.* University of Chicago Press, Chicago, Ill. (2003).
2. John Kenneth Galbraith, *Money: Whence It Came, Where It Went.* Houghton Mifflin Company, Boston, Mass. (1975).

Chapter 3: FDIC Examiners End the "Anarchy of Uncontrolled Banking"

1. John Kenneth Galbraith, *The Great Crash: 1929.* Houghton Mifflin Company, Boston, Mass. (1954).

Chapter 4: Clark Warburton: Pioneer Banking Economist

1. *Clark E. Warburton Collection.* Special Collections & Archives, George Mason University Libraries, Fairfax, Va. (Donated 1979 and 1984).
2. Milton Friedman and Anna Schwartz, A Monetary History of the United States, 1867-1960. Princeton University Press, Princeton, N.J. (1963).
3. Thomas F. Cargill, "A Tribute to Clark Warburton," Journal of Money, Credit and Banking (1981), 13 (1), p. 89.
4. Allan H. Meltzer, *A History of the Federal Reserve.* University of Chicago Press, Chicago, Ill. (2003).
5. Clark Warburton, *Depression, Inflation and Monetary Policy, Selected Papers, 1945-1953.* The Johns Hopkins Press, Baltimore, Md. (1966).
6. Michael D. Bordo and Anna J. Schwartz, "Clark Warburton: Pioneer Monetarist," *Journal of Monetary Economics* (1979), 5 (1), p.p. 43-65.
7. Leland B. Yeager, *In Search of a Monetary Constitution.* Harvard University Press, Cambridge, Mass. (1962).
8. Bray Hammond, *Banks and Politics in America.* Princeton University Press, Princeton, N.J. (1991 and 2001).

Chapter 5: The American Bankers Association

1. Fritz Redlich, *The Molding of American Banking, Views and Ideas.* Johnson Reprint Corporation, New York and London, Volume One (1968), Appendix.
2. Allan H. Meltzer, *A History of the Federal Reserve.* University of Chicago Press (2003), pp. 421-22, 522.

3. Paul B. Trescott, *Financing American Enterprise.* Greenwood Press, Westport, Conn. (1963).
4. Personal Note from Raymond (Skip) Cheseldine to Carter H. Golembe (2007).

Chapter 6: An Intervening Episode: My Quest for the FDIC Chairmanship

1. Arthur M. Schlesinger, Jr., *The Coming of the New Deal.* Houghton Mifflin Company, Boston, Mass. (1959), p. 443.
2. Richard F. Janssen, *Wall Street Journal*, January 8, 1964.
3. Eileen Shanahan, *New York Times*, October 28, 1963.
4. Robert Dallek, *Flawed Giant.* Oxford University Press, London and New York (1948), pp. 34, 111, 114, 118.
5. *Washington Financial Reports*, October 29, 1963.
6. Editorial, *Washington Post*, December 29, 1963.
7. "The Best of Enemies," *New York Times*, June 24, 2005.
8. *The President Recordings: Lyndon B. Johnson – Toward the Great Society (February 1, 1964-March 31, 1964).* Miller Center of Public Affairs, University of Virginia, Charlottesville, Va. (Undated), p. 210.

Chapter 7: The Saxon Revolution and Its Aftermath

1. "James J. Saxon," *The Golembe Reports,* Vol. 1980-2, February 25, 1980.

Chapter 8: Reflections

1. Theodore H. White, *In Search of History: A Personal Adventure.* Harper & Row, New York, N.Y. (1978), p. 406.
2. "Annals of Politics: The Compassion of Lyndon B. Johnson," *The New Yorker*, April 1, 2002.
3. *Report of the President's Commission on Financial Structure and Regulation*, December 1971, pp. 91-92.
4. *The Golembe Reports Twenty-Fifth Anniversary Edition*, 1967-1992, pp. 21-27.
5. "Reflections," *The Golembe Reports*, 2002-4, April 8, 1982.

About the Author

Carter H. Golembe is widely regarded as a leading authority on the banking business and the way it is regulated. He is a distinguished author and public speaker on trends in public policy affecting banking and the financial services industry.

Golembe began his career as a financial economist with the Federal Deposit Insurance Corporation in 1951. He served as Deputy Manager of the American Bankers Association from 1960 to 1966. In 1966, he founded Golembe Associates, Inc., a banking research and consulting firm headquartered in Washington, D.C. When Golembe Associates was merged with BEI, Inc., of Atlanta in 1989, he joined The Secura Group, a Washington-based financial services consulting firm, as Chairman of the Board. For nearly two decades, he served as Executive Manager of the International Financial Conference, a seminar group of U.S. regional bank CEOs he founded in the late 1970s to address multinational banking and financial issues.

Later in his career he became President of CHG Consulting, Inc., in Delray Beach, Fla., and Managing Trustee of the Support Group for Modern National Banking, an organization in Washington dedicated to the enhancement of the national bank charter. He served for many years on the Board of Directors of Barnett Banks of Florida, then the state's largest banking organization.

Golembe was the principal author of *The Golembe Reports,* a series of interpretive essays on major public policy issues that he wrote continuously from 1967 to 2002. He co-authored a college-level textbook called *Federal Regulation of Banking.* He also authored *The Golembe Reports: Twenty-Fifth Anniversary Edition* and co-authored *The Golembe Reports: Key Banking Issues Entering the New Millennium.*

Golembe holds a doctorate degree in economics from Columbia University in New York and a bachelor of law degree from George Washington University in Washington.